The Spy

The Wall

Two Sides

an Autobiography

by

Peter van Wermeskerken

Table of Contents

Dedication

To Käthe, for it was because of her, the whole story began. You, dear readers, do not know her, and it should stay that way. Her real name is a different one. Our friendship has already lasted over sixty years.

Prologue

I'll come straight to the point. I was a double agent, working for the Dutch BVD (Binnenlandse Veiligheidsdienst—Dutch Secret Service; now AIVD—Algemene Inlichtingen en Veiligheidsdienst, General Intelligence and Secret Service) and against the East German foreign intelligence service, the HVA (General Reconnaissance Administration) of the Ministry for State Security (abbreviated Stasi). Many have asked if I found my activities exciting or if I had been in danger.

I can answer both questions with a clear "no." One has to keep a clear mind and be, as a matter of fact, resilient. Boredom and long waiting periods are essential aspects. You have to be able to cope with that. But dangerous? No way. First, the HVA used me. I didn't use them. If they had locked me up in an East German prison cell, it would have meant that when I returned to the Netherlands, I would have been subjected to a thorough interrogation by the BVD. And I would have told them everything I knew about the East German intelligence service. But I was in danger in the Netherlands. In any case, I had "bought myself off" since, after being recruited by the East Germans and accepting their offer, I was given clear rules by the BVD that I had to comply with. Point-blank.

In addition, Walter Ulbricht, Erich Honecker, and his little Margot, whom the people despised, knew how to suppress their people. They had learned how from Russian dictators and Hitler. The intelligence service was utterly harmless. The 3,800 officers of the HVA (there were no troops) came from a grammar school in the GDR, and they had all attended a kind of college for espionage. All HVA staff boasted fervently that, "After the Israeli Mossad, we are the best intelligence service in the world." When I heard that, I could only laugh. What an arrogance! Pride comes before a fall—and that was the case here. Apart from the Federal Republic of Germany, the HVA had little success. That was why I am convinced that the American CIA, the Russian KGB, and even the Dutch BVD were a class above them.

Due to being epileptic and mainly because of the adverse effects of my medication, which I'd had to take since 1946, I unfortunately had no great school career. That changed in 1958 when I went to an agricultural college. Grammar school in 1953 was outside my reach. However, there was no comparison between the Dutch grammar schools and those in the GDR—and probably those in West Germany. Many hours were wasted on communist and political "education" in the GDR. That was how people in communist countries learned to stand up without criticism for the teachings imposed upon them from above.

Those who have yet to be taught to think critically about the society in which they live cannot ask critical questions. This ultimately means an introverted society—a communist society, for example—that discourages creativity and eventually fails. I am convinced communism will ultimately also fail in China, Cuba, and North Korea.

The lushes in the HVA needed to be more clever to deduce that I had changed to the Dutch counter-espionage side. They never once tried to test me. With my character, they would have had little luck anyway, but they needed to have the intellect to ask intelligent questions. Once, they tried to drink me under the table. The attempt failed because, being epileptic, I drank little alcohol—and at that time, none.

This period of my life was interesting, and I gained much experience. People around me feared for me, but I didn't worry. Being Dutch, I was always truthful to the BVD. In return, the service managed me so I was never uncovered on the other side of the Berlin Wall. The impertinence I revealed in my work as a journalist caused much laughter in the BVD.

The football game between Dukla Prague and Ajax took place in March 1967. It was in the aftermath that the HVA recruited me as a spy. Within five days after my return to the Netherlands, the BVD had made me a double agent. Officially, the story continued until September 1970. In the autumn of 1969, because of the insistent pressure from my wife and the fact that we'd just had a son, I informed both intelligence services that I intended to cease my activities. I would have loved to see the faces of the Stasi officials (from a safe distance) when they read the article in the Algemeen Dagblad—the major Dutch newspaper I worked for. The BVD revealed the transgressions of the Stasi with sparing words. I am convinced that my supervisor in Berlin got into trouble. Things became a lot worse for him when, some two months later, another double agent he'd supervised told his story to a Dutch magazine.

During the Cold War, the place was afloat with spies and double agents. The East German intelligence service received high praise in the newspapers. They prided themselves on their successes in the Federal Republic. Their spies were warmly welcomed in West Germany, as were all East German citizens. In this way, the East German Ministry for State Security (MfS) brought Gunther Guillaume into West Germany in 1956. He'd been recruited four years earlier to settle in the heart of capitalist West Germany, in Frankfurt am Main. With his wife, Christel Boom, also a "certified" spy, he opened a coffee shop. In 1957, Günther joined the local Social Democratic Party, SPD.

The West German intelligence service and the SPD should have seen signs then. Even in the following years, someone should have been suspicious when the pair worked their way up in the SPD. But both the SPD and West German counter-espionage failed. In 1968, Markus Wolf, the highest chief of the HVA, recruited Gabriele Gast, a twenty-five-year-old political science student from Cologne, as an agent. In 1973, she got a job with the Federal Intelligence Service and worked her way up to become a director. She was never debunked. Only after the fall of East Germany was she betrayed by an HVA colonel.

Christel Boom also worked as a secretary in the SPD office in Hessen. Guillaume is steadily climbing the career ladder within the SPD. In 1964, he became a full-time party official. He was elected to the municipal council of Frankfurt in 1968, and in 1969, he managed the election campaign of Transport Minister Georg Leber. He put Guillaume into close contact with Willy Brandt and got him a Federal Chancellery (German White House) post.

Brandt made him his secretary thanks to his zeal and organizational talents. There, the spy from the GDR had access to all the Chancellor's secret information and confidential discussions. Only in mid-1973, seventeen years after he'd become a secret agent, did West German intelligence become suspicious. When he was arrested on April 24, 1974, Guillaume said cheekily, "I am an officer of the National People's Army of the GDR and on the Ministry of State Security staff. I ask you to respect my officer's honor."

For Brandt, it was a mitigating circumstance that he was the first West German Chancellor who sought communication with the East German authorities—unfortunately unsuccessfully, as East German leaders Ulbricht and Honecker were far too stubborn to enter talks.

In my time, about fifty thousand people worked for the Stasi, with over 90 percent involved in domestic repression. Under the Honecker's, this number doubled to over ninety thousand oppressors and several thousand clerks. Moreover, at that time, an unprecedented system of one hundred thousand semi-professional informers was set up in the GDR. Each of these domestic spies had about forty informants. That way, the Stasi knew what was happening in almost every family.

... Erich and Margot Honecker...

In my time, about fifty thousand people worked for the Stasi, with over 90 percent involved in domestic repression. Under the Honecker's, this number doubled to over ninety thousand oppressors and several thousand clerks. Moreover, at that time, an unprecedented system of one hundred thousand semi-professional informers was set up in the GDR. Each of these domestic spies had about forty informants. That way, the Stasi knew what was happening in almost every family.

Internal repression is a weak feature of every dictatorship and is associated with many cruelties. The scale of the atrocities that the GDR regime committed against its people, among other things, came from former SS camp guards and interrogators from the Third Reich. Moscow supported this with certain tricks to detect the desired "truth" from its prisoners. That all German war criminals were West German or that they had been sent from the GDR to West Germany was purely a propaganda lie.

The BVD had a dual task: It had to look after me, but it also had to pay attention to those who, on behalf of East Germany, tracked contact between spies and BVD agents. The BVD, therefore, had to know who else was working in the Netherlands as a spy for East Germany.

CORRESPONDENCE CHESS

As an ambitious young chess player, I started participating in international correspondence chess tournaments in the early sixties. The tournaments were helpful in three respects: Firstly, it was fun to play; secondly, I deepened my knowledge of opening theory; and lastly, it was fun to hear exciting things from all kinds of people everywhere. With many opponents in the tournament, I would play a second game. For me, it was about deepening the opening theory in my repertoire. Sometimes, letters of two, three, or even four pages were written—all about one specific move with many variants and sub-variants.

Besides the tournament games, some participants wrote about different topics—with an American missionary in Kenya, for example. I was also in contact with a student in the Uzbek capital, Tashkent, who studied tropical architecture. One day, he asked me to order certain books about tropical architecture in New York and London, which I should send to his university to get his professor's attention. The books arrived after a few months, safe and sound. As a thank-you, he sent me the first three volumes of the four-part series of Russian chess grandmaster Yuri Averbach about the endgame. The books were in Russian, but I found a Dutch booklet with a rough translation. I could understand everything else quite well since the Russian chess moves are written using our alphabet, and one piece can only be on one square at a time.

A correspondence chess tournament had eight participants, usually from East Germany. This was one of their few chances to contact people from the West. These tournaments were in every playing strength. Nowadays, there are chess tournaments on the Internet. But in those days, a tournament took quite a long time—a single game could take up to two years. Thus, the chances were good that the East Germans could learn interesting facts from the West, apart from chess.

Censorship in the GDR was strict, but chess letters were forwarded rapidly. In addition to the postal delay, there was a delay of approximately three days. Furthermore, the post from the East Germans was read by a censor. Therefore, a game of thirty moves took about sixty weeks without the additional delays from holidays.

In one of these tournaments, I had Johann Bosch as an opponent. He worked in the Barkas plant in Chemnitz (former Karl Marx Stadt), which produced light trucks.

One day, Johann asked me in a letter if I knew a young man in the Netherlands or another Western country who would like to correspond with a girl who worked at his company. I thought about it and finally concluded that I could be such a young man. And thus, I wrote my very timid first letter to Käthe. She was almost two years younger than me and had a strong personality. Her letters were not just replies to mine and stories about her life but also German lessons for me. In her opinion, my German was terrible but good enough to understand me.

We exchanged two or three letters a week. Each took a week and a half to get to Chemnitz from Zeist. Käthe had already sent many letters and photos to Zeist, and she wanted to meet me at some point. She could not come to Zeist because the GDR did not allow its citizens to travel to the West. So, I had to find a way to visit Käthe. The GDR authorities were not keen on nosy people from the West, and certainly not journalists. So I had to think of something.

Short biography Margot Honecker

Margot Honecker was born 4-17-1927 in Halle aan de Saale in Saxony Anhalt, near Leipzig. Her father was a shoemaker. She became Minister of Education alongside her husband. Her education went up to the lowest grade in junior high school. In 1945, she became a member of the communist party. She worked her way up in politics with her elbows. In 1950, she became (22) the youngest member of parliament. She met Erich Honecker when he became chairman of the youth organization FDJ in Halle. He was married, and she was the unmarried mother of a daughter, but she seduced him into divorcing and marrying her in 1955. That relationship did not fit with party doctrine. Separately, they were sent to Moscow for a while for re-education. After she returned, her career took off. In April 1963, she became Minister of Education (4 months later, I had an interview with her; see next chapter) and became a member of the Central Committee of the communist party SED. 1971, she was the driving force behind Erich's election as president when he removed Walter Ulbricht from office. After the Fall of the Wall, the Honeckers fled to Chile. Erich returned to Germany to die. Margot died in Chile in 2016.

1. Rdio Report About Youth in the GDR

As a young twenty-year-old, I made contact with Minjon, the youth wing of AVRO, a major Dutch broadcaster. Herman Broekhuizen and Gerrit den Braber, who did radio for children, teens, and tweens, encouraged me to set up a section in Zeist, which I did. My bedroom was the first "studio," with three microphones, three tape recorders, a record player, and numerous tapes with a corresponding amount of material for cutting and fixing. In our department, I usually had ideas for features and documentaries. The most significant success was a festive event, from which the proceeds went to a village for people with disabilities. Initially, we sold thirteen hundred tickets, but ultimately, almost two thousand paying visitors turned up. The biggest attraction was the Royal Navy's steel band.

The heads of departments at Minjon regularly came together in Hilversum to exchange offers. In one of these meetings in late 1962, I suggested we broadcast youth in the GDR. They had been trapped behind the Berlin Wall from August 1961

After a few weeks, we got permission once the executives had discussed and approved the idea. Of course, the program could not contain political propaganda for the East German regime. AVRO gave me a letter of recommendation for the State Radio of the German Democratic Republic. Sound recording devices were not allowed to be brought into the GDR, but that was made available there. After some back-and-forth, dates were created exclusively in Berlin.

...*The Berlin Wall separated neighbors and families...*

Strangely, the East German authorities in 1963 did not care where I would stay. However, it was already clear from my visa application that I would stay in the GDR much longer than necessary to complete the documentary. That was because I wanted to visit my friend Käthe in Chemnitz.

Traveling by train, I took gifts for Käthe and her family. Western and German reading material was contraband, so everything I had hid 'contraband' behind folding seats in the aisles. I also hid some papers in the toilets, which passengers could not enter during the customs inspection stop. For a girl I was in love with, one also takes something gold, such as a necklace. If I had declared this, the officers would have had to cut off 30 percent of the weight as import duties. Money was not accepted as a substitute. The state needed gold to cover the East

German mark, which was stable then. So I had to smuggle the necklace. This can be easy if you look innocent, are friendly to the officials, and show the contents of your suitcase. This way, I didn't have to empty my pockets.

I often studied chess during my train journeys in and through the GDR, especially during inspections. Waiting, waiting, the endless waiting—that was dreadfully boring. A chess book published in the GDR lifted me above suspicion. Moreover, these books cost only half the price of those in the West and were at least as good. West German books and other languages the customs officials could not read, apart from Russian ones, were prohibited.

I had to change trains in Dresden. After half an hour of waiting, I took the little train to Chemnitz. After my arrival, I called the family from the station. As there was no cozy bench to sit on, I sat down on my suitcase. After some time, everything went black—Käthe's hands suddenly covered my eyes! I had not heard her approach. There was a very cordial first meeting. Her father accompanied her when she picked me up from the station by car.

After a warm welcome from Käthe's mother and sister at home, something that would have been unthinkable in the West happened. The first question was: "Do you have a Western newspaper with you?" All of them grabbed a book and a newspaper from my suitcase. I was soothed with coffee, cake, and tasty sandwiches. The main thing was that I kept my mouth shut. Käthe and her mother made sure that I was well taken care of. Meanwhile, all four absorbed everything that was going on in the West like a sponge. What a success those German newspapers and magazines and copies of the (German) Reader's Digest were, all purchased at Amsterdam Airport and the stations in Utrecht and Hengelo!

The family had prepared to delve into the reading material and learn about the West. I heard "ohs" and "ahs!" Deep in the southeastern GDR, there was no chance of receiving Western newspapers, television, or radio stations. The exception was Radio Free Europe from the American sector of West Berlin. That sound was, however, professionally disrupted by the East Germans. Whoever looked for that station in Chemnitz heard a noise, with the news barely audible. If you dared to listen to his propaganda station, you had to expect two "gray mice" from State Security on your doorstep. They invited you to the police station, where you had to surrender the Radio. In addition, your employer was informed that you collected fake info that was dangerous to the state. They also threatened that such so-called subversive activities would impact their own lives and the lives of family members. If you came home from the police, all your neighbors knew where you had been—and why.

After they all calmed down from the excitement of the Western newspapers, the other gifts were next. Of course, the gold chain was for Käthe. Her mother and Angela looked at the rest. Mother grabbed the chocolates so she could conjure them up before the visit of the East German family and friends. However, she could not prevent her husband, a sports doctor, from quickly popping one in his mouth as he gazed lovingly at his wife. Angela was delighted with the silver brooch with rhinestones. And then there were the tights, the Nivea, and other creams and lotions. My mother had helped me choose them (as my wife Marga would later help choose Christmas presents for Käthe). They were also delighted about the copies of the Reader's Digest, which at the time often contained anti-communist articles. Her father warned us that no one should say anything about this outside the house. Much later, I discovered these books would be traveling around the GDR. As far as I know, the family was never connected with them by the Stasi or other state agencies.

GOING TO BERLIN

On a Sunday, Käthe and I traveled by train to Berlin. A man sat down opposite us. I said, "Nice, you joined us. Are you also going to Berlin?" The gray mouse did not make a sound, so I tried again to strike up a friendly conversation. "Are you always so reticent?" The question did not work, either. When the man got out, Käthe sighed with relief. "Peter, what was that all about? Did you not see that the man was wearing a lapel pin of the SED"—East German Communist Party? "If you provoke them, you will be arrested instantly."

"Käthe, I haven't done anything. I was trying to make conversation. I did not notice the pin. Käthe said, "Peter, please shut your mouth to strangers. You can behave like that in the Netherlands, but not here."

Later, back in Chemnitz, I made another mistake. Walking through the city, we saw people holding a collection before a church. "Please cross the street, Peter. Anyone who donates will be photographed and later visited at home."

"No, Käthe, I'll go there now. And in plain sight of State Security, I'll give them a West German banknote. They cannot harm me as a foreigner." Käthe could not get away from me fast enough. In front of the church, I took out my wallet and asked the fundraisers if they would accept West German money. They were more than pleased to do so. Well, visible, I gave them some West German and some East

German money and chatted for a while. Only then did I move on. Käthe did not join me until we had walked a few hundred meters.

"I guarantee you, Käthe, that no one will visit you at home," I said.

"I don't think so, either, because I left you. Of course, they know you come from the West."

In Berlin, we stayed with a police officer who was a friend of Käthe's parents. Understandably, they did not want us to share a hotel room. The officer took a significant risk because giving shelter to someone from the West was forbidden. It was also difficult to put us up because they and their son were in a small apartment.

The following day, we went to the East German Broadcasting Service. We were warmly welcomed there with coffee, and Käthe was also included in the conversation. Then, we worked on the broadcast I had requested. The questions I wanted to ask in various interviews, which I had written in my best German, had been translated into proper German.

My interviewee and I would each get copies. An appointment was planned for each morning and every afternoon," as I was told by my supervisor during that week, "before and after recording, one gets into more detailed conversations. Your interviewees will be truly happy about that."

An appointment was scheduled for Thursday morning with Minister of Education Margot Honecker. Her husband, Erich, was second in command in the GDR and would succeed Walter Ulbricht.

Afterward, the engineer had to record all the interviews on tape. He also had to complete numerous forms to accompany the recordings, which would then pass through East German, West German, and Dutch customs. We could go back on Friday afternoon. Every day, we were given lunch at the broadcast studio.

Because of the excellent weather, an interview was planned at a secondary school in the playground that afternoon. First, I spoke to a teacher who recited propaganda about how great everything was in the good old GDR. Then came pupils A and B with similar stories. Afterward, I held the microphone under the nose of a pupil who had yet to be selected for an interview. The boy's stammer was no longer detectable in the studio in the Netherlands.

———————

In the following days, we visited a Berlin department of the FDJ [Free Deutsche Jugend (Free German youth); the words free and democratic mean the opposite in a communist society], which was said to be comparable to a Scout Association. However, the young people were trained in depth in the party's ideology, and while at school, they only received a general political education. We also visited a venue for young people and the editors of the party newspaper, Neues Deutschland.

The visits to the artists and musicians were fun. Here, I could feel freedom. As Kurt Masur, Music Director of the Komische Oper in East

Berlin, said, "Music is from here and everywhere and from all times; the great composers, except Wagner, were always far removed from politics." There was a keen interest in music, especially classical music, in the GDR. Nowhere else were as many orchestras per person as in the GDR. In almost all genres, the number of composers was enormous. We heard very little about that in Western Europe and North America. But this musical wealth had even led renowned composers and conductors to move from West to East Germany. After the fall of the Berlin Wall, the East Rock became popular in West Germany. For painters and sculptors, the story was different. Their work had to meet strict ideological requirements.

Of course, the most exciting was the Thursday morning conversation with Margot Honecker. We arrived at the Ministry, and a little lady from the press service in a black suit greeted us. Käthe was not allowed to go further; she had to wait at the press service. After a while, a second little lady in a black suit fetched me and my companion, the sound engineer. She introduced herself as a secretary and took us into her office, where she asked us to wait. Then we were picked up by a third little lady in a black suit, also a secretary. My companion asked if all the ladies in the Ministry were small and wore black suits. She replied dismissively, "In my position, this is fitting."

...The Ministry for Education did not exist in the 1960s due to asbestos in the construction.

This time, we had to wait a little longer. The gruff secretary came and asked us to follow her. She let us into the office of a senior lady in a black suit, wearing glasses. She said, "Would you please wait a moment? I will announce your arrival."

After a while, she came back and opened a door. And what did I see? A little lady in a black suit. Pointing with a slight bend of her arm, our guide roared, "Lady Minister Honecker!" The minister stood in front of her large wooden desk in a large office with a sitting area and two simple chandeliers. Standing on the carpet before the desk, we shook hands, and I bowed slightly. I introduced myself, but it turned out to be unnecessary. The minister knew who I was and that I had come to make a radio program in the GDR.

The sound engineer asked us to keep the papers from rustling, something he had never mentioned before. Without my noticing it, we got into a conversation that Margot Honecker controlled.

She asked, "What gave you the idea to make a program in the GDR? Most Western newspapers, Radio, and television stations have not been here for more than a year."

"I'm not concerned about others. I trust my route. I play correspondence chess with several citizens here, and I have a girlfriend in Karl Marx Stadt (Chemnitz)," I said.

"Did your broadcasting company give you immediate approval to make a documentary here?"

I replied, "Seemingly, my arguments were strong enough. I am a fairly curious person; I have that from my father. He is editor-in-chief of a local newspaper."

"What is the political stance of his newspaper? And is your father a political party member?" she asked.

"The paper is for everyone in the town of Zeist," I said. "Therefore, it has no political stance. Neither my father nor I are members of a political party. I even gave up my position at the social democratic newspaper in the Netherlands because, after training, I would have had to join the party."

"What do you think of our system of Marxism-Leninism?" she wanted to know.

"The system shouldn't be the reason for such a sharp division between East and West in Europe. Regarding technical advancements, the GDR is the most modern country in Eastern Europe. Marxism-Leninism's production system is ideal in theory. But I cannot understand why there is only one political party."

"But that is not the case," she said. "Our democracy is structured differently. We have, for example, a farmers' party, a student party, and parties for other sections of the population. As a result, our party is a reflection of the population."

This was followed by her lecture on the supremacy of Marxism-Leninism over capitalism. For me, this mainly was verbosity and blah-blah. But she got this political message on the tape for Dutch Radio.

Now that she had formed an impression of me, she allowed me to start the interview. My questions to her as Minister for National Education touched mainly on youth and education. I could have guessed already after speaking with the teacher—the East German system was naturally better than the West's. Unfortunately, her horizons extended only to the Federal Republic. Prepared, she answered all questions quickly, and the political message was unmistakable. She was determined that the discussion would end in less than the thirty minutes she had allowed. Maybe she thought she would "catch more flies with honey than with a barrel full of vinegar" as she invited us all for a cup of coffee in the sitting area. We drank delicious coffee, which could have come from the West. We continued to talk seriously. Before we left, she told me that I should always be honest with my conscience. Later, I asked Käthe what Honecker could have meant by that, but she did not have an answer.

Five days later, Käthe and I took the train back to Dresden. There, we had to change to a slow train for Chemnitz. At that time, the whole journey took some five hours. The romantic nature of the trip was accented by the fact that it was a steam locomotive, but the passing landscape offered little distraction.

A week and a half later, I returned to the Netherlands. My suitcase was much lighter without the gifts, but now I had the unwieldy cardboard box of tapes. East German Radio had asked me to keep the box open for customs. But they showed great interest in the carton with the recordings and related forms on the border. Two border guards whispered to each other, and then one called an officer, who called a superior. They decided that a border guard with a weapon and a guard dog should be placed on the open door of the compartment, which frightened a lady.

I pulled out my chess set and a chess book. The border officials examined my papers, and the train stopped at the border for two and a half hours. Someone had called the East German Broadcasting Service. They called and calmed the men. But to me, they said a form needed to be included or something needed to be filled in correctly. In short, the blame for the delay lay with the gentlemen in Berlin.

After the train set off at a snail's pace to the West German border control, the lady pressed her lips together. They, too, were interested in the box, but here, the forms seemed to satisfy their needs. When we were in the Federal Republic, the lady wanted to know everything about the contents of the mysterious boxes. I told her what I'd said to the border guards: studio tapes from East German Radio for the Dutch broadcasting service.

As a West German who had visited her sister in Saxony, she thought I spoke with an accent from Saxony—thanks to my girlfriend. I also gave customs a set of forms at the Dutch border, but our men did not seem interested. I scheduled an appointment at home to deliver the tapes in Hilversum to the AVRO.

AFTER ABOUT TEN DAYS, I was called by the AVRO with a request to come to the studio. In the foyer, I was greeted by Herman Broekhuizen and Gerrit den Braber, who said, "Peter, you've brought some interesting interviews. But unfortunately, your interview with Margot Honecker cannot be broadcast."

Why not?" I asked.

"This has been decided by the government, by Prime Minister Viktor Marijnen personally. We've reported the interview internally; it was forwarded to the Ministry of Culture. They wanted a copy, and then the ball started rolling. But we found a solution, right, Herman?"

Broekhuizen nodded in agreement.

I was excited because den Braber was always good for a laugh. "You tell the story of the Minister," den Braber said.

I turned bright red and started coughing. "You know, I don't have the voice for that. I forget everything as soon as a microphone is held before me. And is that even allowed?"

He grinned from ear to ear. "This is not forbidden, and your fear of the microphone is nonsense. None of the tapes show your nervousness. Would you like to hear them again?"

I said nothing. Against large Gerrit, against his voice and his laughter, I could not do anything anyway. Then Herman said, "The fact that your voice could be better is irrelevant. You also do not have to memorize anything. We had the text translated into Dutch and cleaned of any propaganda. You've now just to read the text. Of course, it should be put in your words."

I reread the text with someone from AVRO and changed it where necessary. A few days later, I went to the studio to record the five-minute text—about one A4 page. I entered the studio in good spirits with Broekhuizen and an engineer. There was an enormous microphone, and I was extremely nervous. Four hours later, the story was on tape. One week later, the documentary, some twenty-five minutes long, was broadcast.

2. Dukla Prague-Ajax Amsterdam, 2-1

In March 1967, I took my first international flight from Amsterdam to Prague. For the first and last time, I traveled as a soccer fan. Ajax Amsterdam was playing away from home against the army team Dukla Prague. The game in Amsterdam, which was part of the European Championship Cup, ended in a draw.

After some lengthy calculations, I decided that the least expensive way to visit my girlfriend in Chemnitz involved traveling to Prague as an Ajax fan. There, I intended to watch the game, spend the night in a cheap hotel, and, on the following day, take the train via Dresden to Chemnitz and then return to the Netherlands by train. It was about 20 percent cheaper than a return ticket from Utrecht to Chemnitz.

I'll remember the football game in the Juliska stadium on the outskirts of Prague for a long time. Along with about 300 other Ajax fans, I took the urban train. Then I walked to the stadium, as the receptionist in the hotel had directed. At that time, there were wooden stands with about two thousand seats along the field's length. The changing rooms were below the stands. Around the football pitch, raised platforms needed seating for fans. Opposite the stands was a little hut where beer was tapped in half-litre paper cups. It was a glorious time when fans from both clubs stood around the pitch. It was a small event, with fewer than five thousand spectators. As I learned later, Dukla was not particularly popular in Czechoslovakia, nor with Czech football fans. As an army institution, Dukla had an obligation to become champion at least two years out of three, which meant that Spartak Prague and Slavia Prague lost on purpose now and again, or the matches had to be drawn.

The mood was good as I joined a group of three Dukla fans. We were standing in front of the fence, which consisted of a small iron wire, and up behind was a platform where spectators stood. After getting to know Petr from Holandská, two of our quartet fetched four large paper cups of beer and four dry rolls with greasy sausages. I was never a fan of beer anyway, but the stuff in those paper cups was disgusting, and the cups held half a liter, which was a lot. But I looked forward to the roll and the starting whistle.

In a soccer game, the aim is to score goals. At the end of the first half, Dukla was ahead 1-0, cause for celebration. After the applause, everyone went off to fetch more beer, so it took a while before you had a refill in your hands again. This time, a different pair had to fetch the beer. When I had drunk about half of it, I understood the meaning of the platform. A group of men stood with their backs to the soccer pitch, their trousers and shorts wide open. Down beneath the platform, the weeds flourished.

Ajax would not have been Ajax if it had also scored a goal. In the frenzied applause after scoring, I sipped my beer—not entirely accidentally. The football friends from Prague sang, "Oh, what a pity," or something like that. "But now it is your turn to get the beer and sausages!" When I returned with one of the guys with the new provisions, I discovered that alcohol can be consoling. It does that better than the Dutch cup of coffee, also known as a "cup of consolation." The faces of my friends were aglow when they spied the paper cups and the Dutchman, stinking of beer—it was impossible to carry four such cups through a crowd without spilling some. My companion was carrying the rolls with the sausages. But it didn't matter—we were having fun. After halftime, Dukla was leading 2-1.

This was not due to the skill of the eleven army officers on the pitch, who had never had to touch a weapon. The Ajax left-back, Soetekouw, managed a magnificent own goal that goalkeeper Gert Bals could do nothing about. Cursing and ranting, the Ajax trainer, Rinus Michels, later nicknamed the General, stood on the sidelines. After this beautiful goal, Soetekouw was never allowed to play for Ajax again. This achievement brought me another half a liter of the disgusting cold liquid.

After the game, I chatted with the three Czechs before they brought me to the suburban railway. I returned to the hotel without the Ajax scarf, cap, and the wooden shoes from the farmer's village Bunnik I had worn. We had to raffle them off. All three of them had their eyes on the wooden shoes. Back at the hotel, a hot bath, fresh clothes, and throwing away dirty socks worked wonders.

Despite the many street cleaners, Prague was a dirty city at the time. The plastered walls were gray and messy. The town, now called the Golden City, was covered with smog and dust, like all the other East European cities in winter, from coal-burning furnaces and stoves. The cities' electric works, heavy industry, and immediate surroundings also used much of the brown coal mined in northwest Bohemia all year.

The army of eleven has yet to gain popularity. After the Silk Revolution ended the Communist era in 1989, the club was relegated to the fourth league in amateur football. They no longer play in the Czech capital, but since its fusion in 1996 in Příbram, about 36 miles southwest.

As the Netherlands tourist agency advised, I still had half a day to explore Prague's sights. Czechs start the working day very early, so I was a late sleeper in their eyes. I just managed to make breakfast. Then, I made a list of people I wanted to buy a small present. Nowadays, there are many shops and restaurants for tourists in the Golden City, but that was not the case in 1967.

As a journalist, I was used to simply asking my way around. But at that time, tourists from the West were looked at scornfully. Only a few people were prepared to tell me where I could buy gifts. Everyone feared a Secret Service agent would think they were providing me with information. S hardly managed to finish half of the planned shopping.

Around midday on my second day in the Czech Republic, I took a taxi to Prague's Holešovice train station. There, I took the international train to Dresden. The journey was an absolute delight! The trains in the Czech Republic and Slovakia never travel quickly, particularly at that time. It was a train, just as you would imagine, with a steam locomotive from the CDK factory in Prague Vysocany traveling at the pace of a cart-horse!

At Ustí nad Labem (Ustí on the Elbe), a roadway and the Elbe, a continuation of the Moldau (Vltava in Czech), ran alongside the railway. It looked fantastic, but as the train started to climb the Ore Mountains, it got slower and slower. At the border, somewhere in no-man's–land, it stopped for a few hours. First, the Czech customs checked passports and luggage. Then, a few meters farther, this was repeated by East German customs, but twice as thoroughly.

As the train stood in the harsh sunlight, border guards with mirrors and trained dogs inspected the undercarriage. The interior was also checked thoroughly. As an innocent teen, I was naturally absorbed in my chess books published in Leipzig. Older Dutch citizens could read German well, although they avoided speaking it because of their feelings after the Second World War. My German girlfriend had helped me learn German. That was why I was fine explaining my intentions in the GDR to the customs officers. I had to show the presents to my girlfriend and her family. The official present, a pullover, Nivea, cigars for the father, makeup, tights, and chocolates, were in my suitcase.

When we arrived in Dresden, it was already dark. The 63 miles had taken about six hours. At the central station in Dresden, I had to change to the slow train for Chemnitz. Waiting for an hour and a quarter was dull. At this hour (8 p.m.), the central railway station was deserted. Finally, the train arrived. I got it, and after some time, we set off at a snail's pace through the darkness. The train seemed like a dog that had to mark its territory everywhere.

Three hours after arriving in Dresden, I reached my destination, Chemnitz, at eleven in the evening. I called Käthe from one of two telephone boxes. Then, tired, I sat on top of my suitcase in front of the station again and looked in the direction from which I thought Käthe would appear. This time, I was right. Her stepfather's car had hardly stopped when Käthe ran towards me joyfully.

I had brought presents, but it had been more challenging to bring reading material across the border than the first time. After all, I had crossed two East European borders, one heavily guarded. I did not bring newspapers, just copies of The Best of Reader's Digest in German. Again, after feeding me coffee, cake, and sandwiches, the whole family jumped on them. Everything tasted great after almost twelve hours of fasting.

I packed the reading material in light cardboard and put it on different covers, on which I wrote the titles of German chess books. I was not busted in Prague, and I had disposed of the covers in the hotel in Prague. After Ustí on the Elbe, I'd hid the issues quickly in a compartment far from my seat. The train was nearly empty, which worked out well. I collected the books after the border controls and before a stopover in Pirna.

INITIAL CONTACT

It was one morning, and by the time all the initial emotions subsided, the father told me, "Peter, there is still something serious we have to talk about. Käthe, you tell him."

Käthe began, "Two gentlemen visited me at work. They were from ADN"—the" Allgemeinen Deutschen Nachrichtenagentur, the GDR State Press Agency. "They would like to speak to you on Monday afternoon."

"What do they want from me?" I wanted to know.

Käthe: "That's what I asked, but they wouldn't say."

Her father took over. "We assume they aren't from the press agency but from State Security. The press agency is surely just a cover, Käthe."

"When the State Security people go anywhere, they are always in twos," Käthe added. "Apart from that, they have a certain way of talking and are always dressed in gray. That was also the case with them. They want you to come alone."

"Even if you tell me where it is, I will not be able to find my way," I said.

"That is one of the reasons why I want Käthe to accompany you. And it is also about your safety. If they want to recruit you as an agent, they will regard Käthe's presence as an obstacle. And at the end of the day, Käthe speaks better German than you do." I could not help but grin. "Käthe can tell me what was said if she goes along," the father continued.

"That is right, of course," I agreed.

3. Initial Contact with the Secret Service

I was happy that Käthe accompanied me to the café, where the gentlemen from 'ADN' were meeting me. I would never have found the café alone in the narrow streets in the center of Chemnitz. I saw the inside of a pub for the first time. They offered me a beer. I declined, saying I wouldn't say I liked beer. "Our beer is perhaps not quite as good as your Heineken, but it is not bad," said one man, who introduced himself as Heiner and was in his mid-forties.

I said, "I once tried that awful stuff from Heineken and spat it right out. "Damn, it tasted like bitter dishwater." To this, Käthe, Heiner, and Eberhard Molzan, the youngest man, laughed heartily, maybe because the disgust on my face was apparent. Eberhard and Heiner ordered a beer while Käthe and I got coffee. The men said that they expected me to be alone. I answered truthfully that I would never have found the café without Käthe.

Eberhard came quickly to the point. "We are both journalists. What are your journalistic activities?" I said I worked for the largest regional newspaper in Zeist, a town about 6.5 miles east of Utrecht, which had fifty-five thousand inhabitants. I said that I write about anything: the annual meeting of the Christian Women's Union, a documentary about building aquariums, reports of meetings of political parties, reviews of plays, reports of churches changing pastors, etc. I was known in Zeist and local politics and stuck out like a sore thumb.

Heiner and Eberhard wanted to know more about my education. "It began in kindergarten with Mrs. van Ginkel, about 30 yards from my parent's house," I said, "a little farther away than the butcher Hunnik, where I stood in line during the last winter of the war for my mother at the cook shop. I got deep into details for the next half an hour. It was them, Käthe interrupted me. "Peter, you don't have to go into so much detail."

I turned to her and whispered, "I'll tell them so much they'll get dizzy." And I continued. I managed to go on for the next half an hour, but I was interrupted when I had to ask Kathe for help finding the right German word. It seemed the two Stasi boys hung from my lips, or they pretended. Anyway, I enlarged my explanation for a third of an hour. Käthe nudged me a few times. I understood and put an end to it. They seemed most interested in my career in journalism. That started in January 1961 at Het Vrije Volk (Free People) in Amsterdam, followed by a paper in Delft, a paint lab, the paper in Aalsmeer, and finally, Zeist with my father's paper. I still look back on this monologue with a smile because I was already controlling the conversation and would not let myself be interrupted.

Eberhard had indeed tried, but I didn't even react. That was the only attempt. At the end of my story, they asked me only one question: "When did you do your military service?" But because I was an epileptic, I had never been conscripted. However, I had to come home at some point during the morning from my work on a farm. There, I found my parents drinking coffee with a young lieutenant of the Army Health Service. He already had a letter from my neurologist, Professor Van Wulfften Palthe, who was, at that time, director of the Royal Air Force Medical Center in Soesterberg. For him, I was a research object. I explained this, too, to Heiner and Eberhard in detail. If you want to look at it that way, Eberhard only once interrupted me with a compliment. "Well, the fact that you can describe everything in such detail could benefit our future cooperation."

The time they were passed. Käthe and I had already been sitting in the pub for several hours. The atmosphere became uncomfortable when I asked Ebi and Heiner about their experience as journalists. Käthe said afterward that she had become a little flushed. Eberhard, or Ebi, was about three or four years older than me. Heiner was about 45. By the look of his belly, he had been drinking more beer and participating in less sport than me. I asked them then how long they had been working for the ADN and in which editorial department. They gave only general information. They worked, they said, for the foreign desk. Their news agency did not want to be dependent on Western agencies.". . . because they spread propaganda. But, I said, "UPI, AP, Reuters, Agence France de Presse, and the Dutch ANP are not government offices, as is the case in Eastern Europe. "Ebi and Heiner did not comment.

For them, my remarks were a signal to get straight to the purpose of the meeting. Ebi took the initiative. "Hey, Peter, would you mind writing an article on the Dutch royal family and the importance of the monarchy in Dutch society since the beginning of the twentieth century? We would also love some photos."

"Of course I can," I replied. But I would need at least three weeks. I'm staying another week with Käthe and will send you the article in about four weeks."

"No, no, don't send it," Eberhard implored. "It would be better if you brought it to us here."

I looked at him in amazement. "But that makes the whole thing a lot more costly, both in money and time. Besides my normal work, I need to take three weeks. Of course, this involves costs. And if I must pay another several hundred Marks for the trip, I need a fatter wallet."

"Don't worry about that," Ebi said. What kind of fee do you have in mind?"

"Let me think. Maybe 250 guilders, or about 225 marks."

"For your first report, which is a test, you'll get 150 marks plus travel costs and reimbursement of additional expenses. Write everything down and save the invoices."

"As a start, I agree to 150 marks, but the next one will cost you more. My time and skills must be rewarded."

"That may be the case, but I cannot promise future fees. I'll have to discuss that with others."

Despite this, I tried to put on pressure: "Know what, Eberhard? The 150 marks for the article are okay. But you have to promise me something: Käthe should be allowed to go to the Netherlands should we marry."

Eberhard and Heiner withdrew to discuss this. Some time, I was passed. My question made Käthe flush, for what I said was a significant surprise to her. I had not discussed it with her before. "Was that a proposal?" she whispered.

I said, "Dear Käthe, it was not yet a proposal. It will only mean something when I know that you can come to the Netherlands and that you would want to. But I promise I'll propose if you can leave for the West."

"That is something I have to discuss at home. Perhaps I will apply to leave the country," she said. What Käthe knew, and I didn't: as soon as she made an official application to leave (which she did some weeks later), any chance to achieve anything in the GDR in any way was gone.

Ebi and Heiner returned, and Heiner said, "We cannot give a definitive answer to your question currently, but we can tell you that we will do our very best. In exceptional cases, GDR citizens are allowed to move to the West. We have to clarify your request with our superiors, and they have to send it to the responsible political authority."

"Heiner, I understand," I said, "but you must understand that we all have deadlines. Only after a positive response can I ask for Käthe's hand in marriage, or else I must move to the GDR."

"If you moved here, you wouldn't be useful to us," Heiner said.

Around five o'clock, Käthe and I left the restaurant. "I was ashamed of you, Peter," she said. "You were so brave. Firstly, that is not how we do things in East Germany, and as well as that, you spoke to people from whom you know; I think you understand what I mean." We were walking along the street, so she was speaking softly. "Those people have all the power here." She gave me her arm. "On the other hand, it was enjoyable. However, I feared a car would stop and take us with them the whole time."

"You do not need to fear that, my dear," I said. "Here, I am practically immune. They need me, and I don't need them."

We returned home around six o'clock. The whole thing had taken about five hours, and the family had been worried. The father, mother, and Angela wanted to know everything immediately.

"I feel wary," Käthe said. "As his conversation drew close, Peter mentioned my possibility of moving to the West. "The women, Angela in particular, were overcome with romantic sentiments. However, the father remained unperturbed. Käthe was told to wash her head with cold water to think straight and to think about what she wanted to say about the afternoon's events. I was allowed to add my comments, and the father would dig deeper if needed. The mother and Angela now had no choice but to be quiet. Käthe was and still is a very down-to-earth woman. Nevertheless, she could not report coherently that evening. With specific questions, the father could form a reasonably clear picture of what was discussed in the café.

He had to laugh. "But you did try to press ahead, Peter. Not only do you demand more money, but you also want to abduct a young worker from the Republic!" He did not expect the latter to succeed, even if Käthe applied for an exit visa. "Apart from that, you cannot get married here," the father added, "even if your plans would still be serious. The news would spread like wildfire through the entire GDR. That would mean the beginning of an uprising. They will not allow it. We would be overjoyed for Käthe if she could move to the West. But then we could never see her again. Please find happiness over there, Käthe. But remember that you could not return to your family if things do not work out between you."

The father turned to me. "The conversation was more or less what I expected. They did not put their cards on the table because Käthe was present. That is why they want you to come back to Berlin. They have given you a little piece of work to keep you occupied. When you get home, you should tell your father everything and discuss with him whether you should perhaps inform the authorities of a possible attempt to recruit you to spy for the GDR." I was shocked when I heard the word. "That is what I would advise you to do, as it is your best protection in the Netherlands."

I promised him I would and spent another wonderful week with the family.

4. My Dutch Secret Service "Fathers"

At home with my family, I told them everything about the football game, the beautiful train ride, and the pleasant stay with the Schultz family. Mindful of the words of Father Schultz, I waited until my dad and I were alone that night. Then I began: "Dad, I need your advice on a confidential matter."

Father looked at me and put down his newspaper; he'd had it open to the same page for hours. I told him about the conversations with Herr Schultz and in the pub with the men we suspected were from State Security.

"I'll call the police commissioner tomorrow," my father answered.

"It is better that you speak with him in person. Käthe's father said he thought it better not to discuss this matter over the telephone."

"That is a good idea. I will visit him at a quarter past eight." I warned my father that our colleague, De Wit, would also be there for the police report.

The following morning, my father got an appointment with the commissioner for a quarter past eight. Shortly afterward, my phone at the offices of the Nieuwe Zeister Courant, the local newspaper, rang, and ten minutes later, I walked into the police station.

"So," the receptionist said, "all the editors at the Nieuwe Zeister are visiting us this morning?"

"The commissioner asked me to come," I answered.

"Then hurry; they are already waiting for you."

In the commissioner's office, I met the commissioner, my father, and a security officer from the local police. It was the first time I had met him personally. The commissioner said,

"Peter, by coming to us, you show you are a good citizen. Your father has outlined the events, but it would be better if you go along with Mr. Jansen, the security officer." As I followed Mr. Jansen, I asked him if he had a uniform. He did, but he only wore it when it was required of him. "Perhaps it has become a little too tight since I last wore it," he said jokingly.

I realized that, with him, I was in the right place. He let me speak but explained clearly the details he wanted and what I could omit. He constantly asked me for more information. At some point, he said, "Mr. Van Wermeskerken Junior"—for the first time, someone did not call me Peter to distinguish me from my father — "your story seems so serious to me that I must pass it on to The Hague. So go to work or go home and speak to nobody about it. That includes the police commissioner and the mayor."

The following day, Mr. Jansen called me at home. Father ran to the telephone, lifted the receiver, and then called me to come. I was asked to appear at the police station at two in the afternoon. When I arrived, I was met by Jansen and two men in his office, then Jansen left. The men introduced themselves: The older one was called Van der Deugd, and the younger Van der Niet. "Together we are the Deugniet Duo" (deugen = worth, and niet = less: the worthless), the elder one said, smiling.

Then, he immediately became serious. "I am sure you understand that we are from the BVD. Part of our job is to uncover spies. At the same time, we try to recruit spies to help us understand the methods used in other countries. Currently, we are involved mainly with Iron Curtain countries. We want to know how they found you and why they might have thought you could be useful and loyal to them."

The building of the BVD in The Hague had a jolly number of antennas on its roof.

When he finished, I asked him what he meant by loyalty.

Van der Niet explained: "There are three reasons one would show allegiance to a country's intelligence service. One can feel loyal to one's nationality and people. Then, loyalty can be based on ideology. This is the case with many communists with strong convictions. Finally, loyalty can result from greed when a spy is well-paid. Occasionally, the job can be risky. But first, please let us know your personal history—everything important—within ten minutes." When they were satisfied, I mentioned with a grin that it had taken me almost two hours to tell the same story to the East Germans. They laughed.

They then asked me to explain how I had come into contact with East Germans.

I told him how I had met a colleague of Käthe through correspondence chess about the documentary I had made for AVRO and that I had interviewed Margot Honecker. I said that I had found communism in the GDR so unappealing after my first visit that back in Zeist, I joined the liberal party VVD, I founded a youth division of the VVD and the social democratic PvdA and also a youth parliament, and about my work for the local newspaper.

Van der Deugd made some notes, and occasionally, the two men looked at each other briefly. They questioned me about my second trip to the Dukla Prague-Ajax football game, my trip to Dresden, and the conversations in the pub in Chemnitz. I told them how the unknown men had appeared where Käthe worked and that Käthe had accompanied me to the café at her father's insistence. Van der Deugd and Van der Niet wanted to hear Heiner and Eberhard's exact words. I told them the whole story as best I could recall.

Then followed a few quick questions, some of which surprised me. "What did you bring the family from the West?" I told him I had smuggled some Western books with fake chess covers through two customs checks because I knew the family was interested in reading." The men kept straight faces. "The customs officers at the Czech-GDR border were quiet and polite. Of course, I had earlier studied the schedule, so I knew that the last stop before the border was in Ustí on the Elbe. The train was deserted then, so I hid the reading material a few carriages down behind folding seats. The actual covers I had left the hotel in Prague. After the border crossing, I had to collect them quickly because it was a slow train. I had tested before to see if everything would fit in my jacket pocket. It wasn't enjoyable that people kept walking down the aisle, but it worked.

I also told them I had occupied myself intensively twice with chess as my passport was being checked. My luggage was searched twice, in vain, because the gold jewelry was hidden in the right pocket of my trousers in my handkerchief. "You should never retake such risks," said Van der Deugd, who seemed to be in charge. "I think you've had excellent luck." His colleague nodded, and I said, "Oh."

And that was it, for a start. We agreed to meet again in a week. The police station was too dangerous, they said, and the chances of being seen were too high. Therefore, we agreed on my suggestion to meet at the playground/restaurant, Jagershuis, at the edge of the forest in Zeist.

"And something else," Van der Niet said, looking me straight in the eye. "We talked about three reasons for loyalty. For you, there is a fourth reason: your girlfriend, Käthe. Did they promise you that she could come to the West? We would like to know exactly how things stand between you."

"I don't let myself be led by ideology," I replied, "certainly not after what I've seen in the GDR. I also do not let money be the driving force in my life. I have a good job now, but it doesn't make me rich. I am Dutch. That is where my loyalty lies. Käthe is an important point. But over there, they are on the ball, and the regime will have to come up with an answer."

"Peter," Van der Deugd said, "I won't beat around the bush. You will never get Käthe out of the GDR. And I'm pleased by your honesty." He looked at his colleague and asked, "Are you?" Van der Niet nodded. "Good. We are returning to The Hague now to decide if we will ask you to work for us. Please think over it and discuss the matter with your father. We have heard good things about him."

I still admire my father for how he dealt with life and for his creativity. A journalist by profession, he was also director of the Small Castle Theatre in Zeist, which boasted high-quality acting. Numerous one-act plays were performed under his direction, and he had also written several plays. My mother, a dedicated nurse, had fallen in love with the tall, handsome actor as he played with his group in her hospital. It was terrific to work for him as of March 1965. He had a gift for making people work better and never hurt anyone's dignity; he never showed off that he was "the boss."

During the war, my father was a political prisoner of the Germans. A competing publisher in Zeist, who was a member of the Dutch National Socialist Party (NSB) and a Nazi sympathizer, had ratted him out. During his captivity, he spoke with other prisoners, including many educated men and politicians, who influenced his thinking. In September 1944, he was sent home with TB, so the mother ended up with a sick husband to nurse in addition to three children, who found this all perfectly normal.

My mother was calm at home, the axis around which all family life turned. I'm still convinced that it was only through her presence that we managed so well. Around four each afternoon, Father often felt that he had done enough work and deserved a nightcap. Of course, the money he spent on alcohol made a dent in the budget, so we were short on cash, and my parents sometimes argued about it. The family prosperity was only boosted when our children started working in the early sixties.

My sister was always at work. She was also in the swimming club and led a group of Boy Scouts. She was only at home to eat and sleep. My sister is creative, just like my father and her aunt. She decorated shop windows and still draws and paints. She has done handicrafts and weaving for decades and is even chairing the National Weaving Association. My brother worked as an accountant and studied, too. Now he devours book after book (mostly history) and newspaper after newspaper.

———

That night, I revisited my father. My sister was working, and my brother was studying upstairs. Mother sat down with us, and I told them about the conversation with the BVD. The acronym BVD alone sent shivers down my mother's spine. She was frightened, and even more so when I told them that the BVD had heard good things about her father. Father beamed. "You see, I'm praised far and wide."

When I told them that the people in The Hague wanted to discuss whether they would let me work for BVD, my mother said, "Oh, please, you are not going to do that, right?"

One of the biggest fears people have when unfamiliar with espionage is that a foreign intelligence service could expose a family member or loved one. This fear was heightened when the service was the notorious East German HVA. People feared that their loved ones would land in prison or, worse yet, be sent to a rehabilitation camp. Stories of torture were familiar.

Father often spoke with Mother on weekends in the first few months to reassure her. She was distressed about her "little man." She cared intensely for me since my epilepsy was diagnosed when I was five or six.

Father often spoke with Mother on weekends in the first few months to reassure her. She was distressed about her "little man." She cared intensely for me since my epilepsy was diagnosed when I was five or six.

A few days later, we received a phone call from The Hague. "Tomorrow at two o'clock at the agreed place," was the message. Even later, the calls were always kept short, too short to be traced with available technology. At the agreed-upon place, I saw the men sitting in the car. I quickly sat with them. "There's too much going on; we must get away from here," Van der Deugd said. I suggested we go into the forest, but the men wanted to maintain sight of their car. I took them to a path that led to Camp Zeist.

I sat one beautiful spring day in March 1967 on a bench between two BVD men. Opposite us, on the grass verge, was the car. "We just passed a restaurant—is the food good there?" Van der Deugd asked. I said that Oud London was excellent, but I could not afford to eat there. Van der Niet asked Van Deugd about his wife's cooking. "Outstanding," he replied, "otherwise, I wouldn't have married her." Van der Niet: "All you think about is good food.

"Peter," Van der Deugd went on, ignoring Van der Niet, "we want you to continue to maintain contact with the East Germans as a member of our service. I assume you have discussed this with your father."

"Yes, I did talk to my parents about it," I said. "I'll do it, and thank you for your confidence. But where do we go from here?"

Van der Niet: "You already have your initial assignment and have agreed upon a fee. The money and reimbursed travel expenses you must give to us. They used the envelope to give it to you. It is blood money, and you may not keep a penny. Never. We've recruited you, and you will receive a monthly stipend." He then gave me a set of instructions. What I earned from the BVD I would not declare to the tax office. I had to copy all my receipts and expenses for working with the BVD. They kept the copies; the originals went to East Berlin. The costs would be reimbursed as soon as possible, also in cash. I had to give all articles, photos, and documents that I collected and took to Berlin one week in advance to the BVD. They decided then what exactly was or was not to be taken to the GDR. "You will carry out the orders of the East Germans for us."

They required absolute honesty and loyalty from me. "Do nothing we don't know about. We'll find out sooner or later," Van der Deugd said. I interrupted him. "That's precisely what they told me in Chemnitz."

He went on. "Never note what you have seen or heard on the way home. Don't talk to anyone about what you did there." They advised me to let the East Germans talk as much as possible. While I could ask mildly critical questions and ask for more detailed information, I had to stay out of it as much as possible when they spouted political propaganda. "They will gently try to win you over by brainwashing," they warned me.

Finally, Van der Deugd said, "We'll always meet with you a few days after your return, and you'll give us your envelope, and we'll give you your pay. You'll tell us everything you've discussed with your East German contacts, where you were, and what you did. Always keep a good eye on your surroundings. We want to know about all of that."

"That's all?" I asked.

"That's all for now," Van der Deugd replied.

"You were too vague about what I should do on the journey home," I said. "If someone asks me what I did in East Germany, I must answer directly. I'll say that I visited friends. If they ask further, I will make up something."

5. Do You See the Girl Flirting with You?

I reached Berlin at the beginning of April with an article on the Dutch royal family in my bag, supplemented with documents about the position of the monarch in society.

The work was anything but easy. It had taken much more time and effort than I had imagined. Perhaps somewhat naively, I had expected a reward for the additional work.

Eberhard had told me it was better to get off the train at Berlin Zoological Gardens and then change to the underground to Friedrichstrasse. From there, it was some ten minutes on foot to the East German border guards. When I returned to Friedrichstrasse in October 2011, I learned why the GDR authorities had chosen this as the border railway station. It is vast, with two underground lines on two levels, a station for regular trains and one for suburban trains. Berlin is widely spread out, and there are few very tall buildings. At street level, there are large department stores. Friedrichstrasse was one of the few crossing points between East and West Berlin. Despite that, it was relatively quiet, for few Westerners wanted to risk a look at the East. One did not visit the GDR for pleasure. If one wanted to stroll and have a leisurely cup of coffee, the Kurfürstendamm in the West was a much better choice.

One significant disadvantage of this lack of activity was that officials had lots of time to check your papers and asked at length why you wanted to visit the GDR. There were always two, at least. I saw Ebi standing behind the passport control. When I had the day pass in my hand (a stamp was not made in my passport), I could greet him. He immediately promised he would make sure that, in the future, I would get through more quickly.

Together, we went to the East German side of the underground and got on a train. After passing a closed station at the next stop, we got out at a small square (later, this turned out to be the Hausvogteiplatz), and once again, we went into a pub.

It must have been a Stasi pub, as evidenced by the cheap, sour beer, the smell of lousy cigarettes, and the place needing to be cleaned better. They had a dark and light beer. Curtains hung in the windows, and it was dimly lit. Almost without exception, the customers were men sitting in twos or threes at tables. Voices were muted. Even then, the pub was filthy and no longer exists today. In 2011, a large building was constructed where it once stood, with shops on the first floor and apartments above. In the pub, I had to surrender my day pass. "For your return trip tomorrow, you will get a new one stamped on Sunday," Ebi promised. His well-built friend, Heiner, whom I had already gotten to know in Chemnitz, later joined us. Then, we got down to business. I delivered my article with the photos, and Ebi and Heiner whispered to each other. I apologized for my imperfect German. I could hear Käthe's critical remarks in the back of my head. But they were delighted. "It only needs a few corrections. You write Dutch German, but it is better than expected," Heiner said.

I received instructions for my new task, and it quickly became apparent that we were departing from journalism. But every remark about that was immediately dismissed. Thinking of the advice of my supervisors in the BVD not to ask overly critical questions, I kept my opinions to myself. Ebi and Heiner wanted me to do some research in the Defense Ministry in The Hague. This wasn't on the beat of an editor for a regional newspaper in the middle of the Netherlands unless there was a connection to military activities in the Zeist area. But I knew the former minister of defense, Piet de Jong. He had defended the political opinions of NATO in the Youth Parliament in Zeist at a very well-attended meeting I had chaired. And I knew Henk Vredeling, a member of the Tweede Kamer (Parliament, comparable to the British House of Commons or US House of Representatives), a defense specialist for the social democratic PvdA. With his help, I founded the Youth Department of the PvdA in Zeist; otherwise, there would have been no discussion partner for the Liberal youth wing, which I had also established, as well as the Roman Catholic KVP youth.

A new government was elected in the Netherlands in early April 1967. Ebi and Heiner now had a great interest in the budget of the Ministry of Defense and the sections in the coalition agreement regarding this ministry. To my surprise, I was asked to write an article and bring documents on which that budget was based. I explained that they would not need an article if they had the documents. Perhaps I only needed to describe the differences between the budget presented in September 1966 and the new plan in an article. This idea was met with enthusiasm, which made me happy because I would not have to do double work. I could easily read about these differences in the national newspapers.

Then, they followed endless security instructions, and when they were done, they went through them again from scratch. When they were about to repeat them for the third time, I interrupted, "I'm a relatively smart person. The repetition is unnecessary, even tedious." This peeved them, and they explained why they thought repetitions were necessary. "It's about your safety, Peter!" I said I could still best provide my security in the Netherlands, but this made no impression on them.

The instructions contained two core points. First, how to acquire the desired information in the Netherlands without risk. Second, the safest way to travel to the GDR. I had to choose a different route to Berlin every time. They would then ensure nothing was stamped in my passport, as had been the case earlier. Western security services could not see how often I traveled to the GDR. "If they know, they'll follow you. If that happens despite everything, we will notice quickly enough. We may call you right back here," Heiner said.

"And how can you know from 300 miles away that I'm being followed?" I asked.

"Because, unlike you, we're experienced and have many contacts." They meant contacts through the embassy in The Hague. We concluded in the early afternoon with a pub pork meal with beans and beer. During the dinner, I had to hand over my expenses calculations, including my fees and travel expenses. I was then given an envelope with 350 West marks.

"You cannot use this here," Ebi warned. "Sometimes, people will ask you to change West marks. If you do, you'll be liable to prosecution, so don't do it." My fathers in the BVD had already told me this when they told me I had to hand over the envelope to them. The BVD would then pay me.

At the end of the afternoon, I wanted to begin my journey back home. Heiner had already said goodbye, but my schedule did not match Ebi's plans. "You cannot easily get home now anyway, so I'll show you Berlin." Without a day pass for the return trip, I had no choice. We walked, and only Eberhard spoke, just spitting out propaganda. Then we arrived at the Brandenburg Gate, and I saw the hated Wall for the first time. "You Westerners are allowed to go to the Wall. Just show your ID card," he said.

"There is no need to be accompanied by my colleague," said a sympathetic Volkspolizist. "If you like, I'll give you a little ladder. Then you can sit briefly up the Wall, and I'll take a photo of you," he grinned. I was shown the photo a month later but was not allowed to keep it. They said a picture of me on the Wall would have aroused suspicions with the police and intelligence service in the Netherlands. Interestingly, they never said "BVD," just "intelligence service."

The weather was gorgeous. There were few Trabis, with their two-stroke engines and stinking exhaust to spoil the setting sun and gentle breeze. "We have to go to the Center (in Berlin, traditionally Friedrichstrasse) because I know a good place to eat," Ebi said. "Shall we take the underground or walk?" I wanted to walk because then you could see so much more. It is always worthwhile to visit a foreign city. We soon arrived at the restaurant. I don't remember what Ebi ordered, but I decided on what the menu called "nutritious sauerkraut," one of my favorite dishes. A rich sauerkraut consists of at least two sorts of meat, with several toppings like raisins, apples, and some fresh herbs. My mother did not like it, and my wife did not either. I've got to find it in restaurants. After all the beer in the pub, I decided to have the GDR equivalent of a Coke. We talked a little about "security."

"Let's go to your hotel first," Ebi said after he paid. It was a simple hotel across from a square with trees, which I recognized later as Hackescher Markt. At the front, where there were no large trees, was a large beer garden. Behind the terrace and along the road were a row of toilets. Loudspeakers hung from trees, which brightened the mood with music. Eastern rock music was unknown in the West but was at least as good as West German, British, or American pop. You can still find this music on YouTube (Ost or East Rock). On the terrace were dozens of tables and chairs, and people were dancing under the trees. It was packed. We found a free table. I looked around. These were the GDR's best years, so I saw relatively well-dressed young people happy and laughing.

People came and sat down at many tables, but not at ours. Maybe I looked like I was from the West. It wasn't desirable to be seen with people from the West. Or perhaps it was because of Ebi; East Germans could always "smell" who was Stasi.

"Don't you want to dance?" Ebi asked.

"Better not," I replied. "My partner has to be able to dance well and lead; otherwise, it turns out to be a disaster, as it was in dance class," I told him how I had been wearing new shoes in dance class.

...The square before Berlin rail station, Hasckescher Markt, has always been cozy in Berlin...

My dance teacher, 6 feet 8 inches tall, was trying to teach me the English waltz. I slipped, and we slid from one corner of the ballroom to the other. Although my teacher fell on top of me, he was injured, not me. After that, I never had to dance; my presence sufficed.

"It only worked with a girl who had participated in a national ballroom championship. She knew me and guided me very well," I said. Ebi laughed heartily.

THE GIRL, GUDRUN

We were silent. Then Ebi said, "You see the girl flirting with you?" Flirting in German is liebäugeln, which was unknown to me, so I asked what he meant. "She is looking at you longingly. Yes, yes, she's even waving!" I looked but saw nothing. "Oh, she just raised her arm. Look there, the girl with the purple sweater!" I could see no girl with a purple sweater. "I'll go over to her," Ebi said. I tried to follow him with my eyes, but the little man got lost in the crowd.

At that moment, a young man asked if he and his

My girlfriend could join me. I told him my friend would pick up a girl in a purple sweater. They both left.

Then, unexpectedly, a young woman in a purple sweater, black skirt, dark hair, and a healthy, vibrant face came towards me with Ebi in tow. She smiled. "So you're Peter from Holland? I'm Gudrun, and I've always lived in Berlin."

I wanted to shake hands, as was appropriate because I didn't know her. But she took my hand and pulled me over to kiss me. If she can, then I can, I thought. I enthusiastically responded to her kiss, first on her nose and then her mouth. "Where were you sitting?" I asked.

"There. . ." She pointed about ten rows over.

"You saw me from there?" I asked in disbelief.

"I already saw you when you both left the hotel and crossed the street. I almost stood up so I could see you better. I winked at you, and then I waved."

"Pity, I saw nothing, but I like your face. We both have brown eyes."

"Foreigners from the West are different. Their clothes and behavior. That's why I noticed you."

Eberhard offered to fetch three beers. "Fine," Gudrun and I sang to the same tune. Ebi had hardly left when she bent forward and whispered, "Is he Stasi?"

I nodded and whispered, "I think so."

"Come," she said, standing up and taking my hand. I stood, and she pulled me. We left the beer garden, the counter, and the dancing couples behind and began running. I hustled to keep up; I've always needed to improve as a runner. We ran past the toilets as fast as possible, then beneath a railway underpass. We smiled at each other like two teenagers who were up to mischief. At the underpass, we turned right. We crossed a smaller square and turned onto a road. We recovered from the run and embraced and kissed for the first time. "Peter," she whispered, "I'm married but want to take you home. It's very close."

"And what about your husband?" I asked.

"He's not at home. He works until twelve, and anyway, he finds nothing wrong with it. When he comes home, he is tired. He's a lot older than me."

"And what's Eberhard going to do with all the beer?" I asked. "I don't care," Gudrun answered. "If he lost you, it's his problem. I want you."

Gudrun was slightly smaller than me and of similar stature. She told me she worked in a bakery. I told her I was a journalist and wrote for a local newspaper. We were comfortable, and we walked arm in arm. I was twenty-seven, and she was a year or two older if I recall correctly. There had been so much going on in the Hackescher Markt earlier, but now the streets behind the station were deserted. As a car drove by, she immediately pulled me into a doorway. She looked at me with a mischievous smile to say, "I've got you!" and pressed against me. I stroked her soft hair—a kiss. I even dared to let my hand wander under her top, my hand gently rubbing her back. She sighed. "I want you," she whispered again.

Then she said, "Just a little farther. I live on this street." Her building had no elevator, so we took the stairs to the third floor. She opened the door and closed it behind me. "We leave the light off; otherwise, it would attract attention from outside," Gudrun said, grinning. I ran after her into the kitchen. Light filtered through the windows from the street.

"Would you like some cake? I bake a cake every Saturday afternoon when my husband is at work. I always try to make a fresh cake. And what would you like to drink? Coffee, tea, cocoa, beer, or a soda?" She immediately set to work.

I never refuse a piece of cake," I said. "I love sweet things."

"Oh, one can bake a perfect pie here!"

"What do you want to drink, Gudrun?"

"I'll take the same as you," she said.

"What kind of cake is it?

"A sort of chocolate tart. I mixed a little liquor into the dough."

"Then no cocoa or beer for me," I said. " I would prefer a coffee."

"Then I'll cook coffee.

"Dear Gudrun, don't let the water for the coffee come to a boil. It makes the coffee bitter. Let it almost come to the boil."

"What do you know about making coffee?"

"That's what my mother always says."

Gudrun cut the cake and placed it on a cake plate. The coffee was bubbling in the coffee pot. I sat down on one of the two chairs. Gudrun came to me and took a cozy seat on my lap. That made the kissing quite lovely. While we kissed, she took my hand and guided it to her chest. I already knew she was not wearing a vest, but now I found she was also not wearing a bra. I gently caressed her breast with my fingertips and then took it firmly in hand. "Nice," she whispered in my ear, kissing me. I stroked the beautiful, soft, warm skin on her back.

Suddenly, she stood up, looked at me, and said, "I have to see to the coffee." But instead, she slowly pulled off her sweater. The light from the streetlamps let her breasts bathe in a warm, velvety light. Then I saw nothing more because she pulled off her top and threw it over my head. When I took it from my face, I watched her go to the stove, her torso naked.

She came back and put the cups in front of us. She stopped in front of me, supporting her breasts with her hands. "My dear Peter, you don't find them too small?" she asked.

"Gudrun, your breasts are wonderful. I don't like big boobs, and yours are beautiful, with the nipples pointing straight."

She sat on my lap again, and we ate our cake and drank coffee. We whispered, cuddled, kissed, and tousled each other's hair.

I'd always told Ebi, Heiner, and the men of the BVD that we just drank coffee and talked in the kitchen. Nothing else. Both sides had said to me that a secret agent takes a significant risk if he sleeps with a strange woman. I agreed, of course, although 007 knew very well how to combine business with pleasure under the sheets. Later in the evening, we were looking fresh after a change of clothes and combing, and we met Gudrun's husband. When Gudrun heard the key in the door's lock, she turned on the kitchen light while we enjoyed our second or third piece of cake. Her husband was excellent in his late forties, maybe early fifties. His twelve-hour shift in a power plant was over.

Gudrun made him something to eat quickly. The man could eat a lot, although it did not show on him. He said there was a search operation in the area. Gudrun laughed out loud and pointed to

Me. "They're looking for you, my dear Peter. They're sure to knock on the door here!" Her husband looked at me questioningly. I nodded cautiously because Gudrun had her arms around my neck, and I wondered what he thought about that. Gudrun was still laughing. "A little man from the Stasi even introduced us!"

Soon, there was a knock at the door, and Hermann opened it. Three men, Ebi up front, came in. "Whore!" he shouted and tried to hit Gudrun, who escaped nimbly. I placed myself in front of him and told him my opinion. "Listen, Comrade," I said, deliberately choosing a communist term, "insulting this lady by calling her something she's not going too far, and just because I prefer her company above yours. I demand that you apologize on the spot!"

To everyone's astonishment, Ebi apologized. Before he pulled me out of the apartment, Gudrun hugged me again and said, "Thanks for everything." She kissed me and whispered, "May I ask another question? Next time, would you please bring me a purple bag that matches my top?"

I grinned. "If I find one, I'll bring it to you."

On our short walk to the hotel, Eberhard scolded me loudly: "You even came here on your account, and then you ran away! I'd been looking for you for hours!"

"Eberhard," I replied, "you showed the dog the bone, and this is what happened. And now everything is fine; you found me."

Ebi said, "I'll pick you up tomorrow morning at the hotel, and until then, do not step out of the door!" After Eberhard got me back to the hotel, I didn't say a word. Gudrun had warned me that it was probably a Stasi hotel and every room would be bugged.

━━━━━━━━━

I did not finish breakfast the following day when Eberhard and Heiner were ready to take me to the border control at Friedrichstrasse. First, they gave me a dressing-down and asked again what I had discussed with Gudrun. They were startled when I said I'd promised to bring her something from the Netherlands next time.

"Peter, you've got to put her out of your head; otherwise, everyone in her circle will know she has a friend in the West. That's not good for her, and others would be suspicious of her," Heiner said softly.

"Heiner," I replied, just as softly, "I promised something. Promises are kept. Besides," I bluffed, "it won't be others who look at her suspiciously, only the authorities."

"Good," he replied. "You can give her something.

Inconspicuously. You can hand it over to her, and then we disappear." Ebi took me to the Friedrichstrasse underground station. From the Western side, I could reach the train quickly.

However, this wasn't allowed because I'd be too conspicuous coming from the West, perhaps a suspected agent. The East Germans often spouted such nonsense. Later, I heard that the CIA watched the station. The East Germans and the Americans had many people tasked with keeping an eye on border crossings in Berlin. Still, staff shortages in the West always occurred after the Wall was erected. Before that time, workers would cross from the city's eastern part daily. Production had to continue, and the logistics had to be well organized for storing reserves in a town of two million inhabitants. East Berlin at that time had five hundred thousand fewer. The West Germans were busy with their economic miracle, so no people were available for border surveillance.

Ebi had to stop about ten yards in front of the East German border guards. Because Stasi had priority, he stepped over to see a few people in a small room and spoke to the security guard. I got a day pass, which I handed to the guard when I showed my passport. Then, I reached the West Berlin underground, which brought me to the Zoo station for the train to Utrecht.

I met my "Fathers" from The Hague in the former restaurant Dijnselburger Corner on the old road from Utrecht to Amersfoort. We met there often after that because it was a good place for business lunches. It was quiet, and there was plenty of space between tables for privacy. Van der Niet and Van der Deugd bombarded me with questions about the journey, the border crossing in Berlin, and if I had seen the day pass (no, I didn't pay attention). They wanted to know how I had been received on the other side of the border.

I had to tell them about the underground journey and the exit at the second stop at that little square (I didn't know its name) about the pub. They laughed themselves silly when I told them that I sat on the Wall and a photo was taken that I wouldn't be allowed to bring to the West. They were interested in the hotel and wanted to know if I'd found a camera or listening devices. I replied that, on Gudrun's advice, I had yet to search for anything.

"Who is Gudrun?" said Van der Niet immediately."

"A young woman Ebi introduced me to on the square opposite the hotel."

"Was she also Stasi?"

"No, she works in a bakery.

"How do you know?"

"That's what she said. She said she bakes a cake every Saturday afternoon. I saw how she took it out of the oven, and I tasted it."

"Were you at her house?"

"We shook Eberhard off at the beer garden. That was fun."

"What did you do?"

"Nothing special; we laughed, talked, ate cake, and drank coffee."

"What did she say to you?"

"She was having fun and wanted me, but she was also married."

Van der Deugd had a film running through his head. He laughed. "Did she get you into bed?"

I replied that I'd already answered the question about our activities.

"How did Eberhard find you?" Van der Niet asked.

"They were with people who went from door to door in the neighborhood. Eventually, when Gudrun's husband was home, they rang the doorbell."

"What was her husband's name? And what kind of work does he do?"

"His name is Hermann, and he works in a power plant," I said.

Van der Deugd studied the menu and ordered a light lunch with coffee. He leaned over and softly asked Van der Niet, "Have we created a new spy who escapes despite all the good advice?" He couldn't stop laughing.

His colleague wasn't so amused. "We must be sure that all goes well, and I don't like this foolishness."

I said that Eberhard had called Gudrun a whore and had tried to beat her. I also noted that Gudrun had asked if Ebi was Stasi. Van der Niet wanted to know how I had answered.

"I said it was likely."

Eberhard and Heiner scolded me. This was the first and last time at the hotel, an experience we would not like to go through again.

They were not pleased when I said I had promised Gudrun a gift next time. "Did she ask you for anything?"

"Yes, a purple handbag to go with her top."

Van der Deugd said, "Well, it's not easy to find such a bag."

"Close by, in the center of Zeist, is a good leather shop, Bonnier," I said.

"It will not be cheap," Van der Deugd said.

"I have no idea," I replied.

I handed the envelope with the Stasi money and got an unmarked envelope with 350 guilders. I signed the receipt and said, "This is a good exchange rate for you because the mark is worth more than the guilder."

Van der Deugd pointed to his inner pocket, where he had put my envelope. "For you, it's not worth anything here, remember?"

Meetings with the "Worthless Duo" were much fun. Van der Deugd and Van der Niet are the spy supervisors. Usually, after we finished our business, we had heated discussions. Incidentally, I eventually had much trouble getting reimbursed by the BVD for Gudrun's handbag. I'd also tried the Stasi. Although Heiner and Eberhard usually had no difficulty paying me, they would only pay for the bag if I had receipts.

6. Stone through window University

It was early May 1967, much more relaxed and cloudy than a month ago. I came to Berlin by plane this time, from Düsseldorf to Tempelhof. This Berlin airport is in the middle of the city and closed in 2008. On landing, we flew onto the runway across a street between two rows of apartment buildings. From the airport, I came quickly by subway and tram to Friedrichstrasse's subway station.

On the east side, I took the subway and got off at the second stop, Hausvoigteiplatz. The brown Stasi pub was located in this shabby neighborhood. Ebi and Heiner were already waiting for me. It was about ten or eleven, and I didn't feel like beer yet. They already had one on. Ebi said we were going elsewhere in Berlin. I would not stay in the hotel again. I protested and said I had brought something for Gudrun, as I had told them last time. Ebi pretended to have forgotten.

What is that, then?

A purple purse that matches her sweater.

Do you have to give it now?

She'll be working now; tonight is best.

Ebi ordered Heiner not to drink anymore. He replied, "He can give it now, or he will go there tonight in a car with a driver. Let's do it now. Do you know where she works?" I replied that she worked in a bakery shop not far from there. "But then everyone sees that he brings something from the west," Ebi remarked. Heiner suggested driving to the store. Eberhard would tell Gudrun I was there. He should then schedule an appointment for Gudrun and me to see each other briefly that evening.

We parked diagonally opposite the bakery shop. Ebi walked to the store; I had to stay in the car. Gudrun came out, and the little Secret Service guy said I was in the car and had something for her. They agreed that she would be in the square at half past seven. She looked at me and smiled but didn't wave.

We drove to Karl Marx Allee, which turns into Frankfurter Allee east of the Frankfurter Tower. The buildings became thinner, and we were clearly in a suburb of East Berlin. We took a few turns and finally came to a detached house.

I looked at the surroundings well, as the Deugniet duo had expressed that their BVD was interested in a precise location. I always wondered whether they knew about the Stasi pub on Hausvoigteiplatz. I could see some large radio towers some distance away from the house. The BVD men asked so much about it that I thought they couldn't place it. Two older adults lived in the villa. The man got along well with Ebi and Heiner, but I rarely got to see the two.

The residents of the house took care of our food and drinks. It was wet: two crates of beer and a few bottles of vodka for us. To my delight, there was also much bread without butter, topped with greasy sausage and cheese. Ebi and Heiner were trying to drink me under the table that first time. That would have been easy because I hardly ever drank alcohol. On the one hand, because of my epilepsy, on the other hand, I've always found driving and work (including espionage), just like sport, incompatible with alcohol.

I drank more beer and vodka that day than I used to. But I also ate half the bread with greasy sausage as a counterbalance. In addition, I regularly drank water just from the tap.

Around noon, Ebi and Heiner told me that Käthe would not get an exit visa. I pretended to get furious because I couldn't show that Father Schultz and the BVD had already estimated Käthe's chances at zero. I walked out of the house, angry. I quickly shook off little Ebi and stout Heiner and walked around in an unfamiliar environment. At an official-looking building, I angrily threw a stone through a window. As soon as I turned around, I was already in a police car.

At the police station, I fulminated against the Volkspolizei officers for not keeping the promise that Käthe would be allowed to come to the Netherlands. In an interrogation room, I spoke briefly with a friendly officer, who calmed me down with a quiet conversation and a cup of coffee. He went away for a while, and when he returned, he asked, "What are we going to do with you now?" Chess, I replied. The best man took out a chess set and pieces. "We have to wait now," he said. My passport was confiscated.

We had an excellent chess game until Eberhard came in with my passport. The officer, however, thought we were not yet ready with our game and asked Ebi to wait a while. The Stasi officer learned this: "A while" does not necessarily mean "a while" for chess players. Only on his second return we ended the game in a draw.

Eberhard concluded very dryly: "Everything is settled. I understand that you are disappointed with what we said to you, but we've got to be honest." Together, we thanked the officer. Eberhard told me that the intelligence service would reimburse the window in the car back to the villa. The building where I threw a stone through the window was part of the famous Humboldt University (probably the Faculty of Agriculture). The main buildings are at Unter den Linden.

We were back at the villa around four o'clock. Eberhard immediately fell for the beer. Heiner had already quenched some of his unrelenting thirst during our absence. I went to the bathroom, put my head under the tap, and drank water. When I returned, Ebi and Heiner resumed their instructions. Through the window, I noticed that it had started to drizzle.

It was close to seven o'clock that evening when I asked when we would leave for the square. "We're not going. You ran away this afternoon, and we must make up for that time," said Ebi. Heiner added that he and Ebi had drunk too much to drive. I got up and picked up the package for Gudrun and my raincoat. "Then I'll walk over there," I said. That sounded firm enough to convince the men that I was serious. Heiner went to a phone down the hall and asked for a taxi.

After a while, a car came, probably from the intelligence service. Ebi walked over to the driver, talked to him, and motioned for me to get in. The driver turned out to know where to go. The ride passed without words.

An already drenched and cold Gudrun stood under a tree on Backbencher Market. She was wearing a plastic raincoat without a hood. She had turned up the collar, but her beautiful hair hung in wet wisps about her head, and the rain dripped through her head under the coat. When I got out, the driver hurried to tell me to give the package and return immediately. Ebi had told him so. That didn't bother me. I saw Gudrun, wet and cold. It couldn't have been warmer than 8 degrees, and she had been waiting for half an hour.

I pulled my raincoat over her head, and we kissed. "I'm so cold," she shivered. She chattered. I walked over to the driver and told him I wanted to take care of Gudrun first, and he wouldn't have to come back until the following day when Eberhard and Heiner had slept off their daze. He protested, but I smacked the car roof with my palm and strode away resolutely. That convinced him he was nothing more than a driver and courier.

I was wet now, too. I put my arm around Gudrun, and we ran as quickly as possible to her flat. I helped her open the door. I took off her raincoat, shoes, and socks in the hall. The water was up to her shoes, and she was cold through and through. "Dear Gudrun," I said, "I will take you to the bathroom, and then you will shower." First, I mixed the water until it was lukewarm. Then, I also undressed and got into the shower with her. I asked Gudrun to put her arms around my neck. That girl felt cold—freezing. Slowly, I increased the temperature of the shower. Slowly, her grip on me tightened. She recovered. After about half an hour in the shower, Gudrun had recovered enough, and she started thinking about kissing again.

At her request, I washed her hair. Then she asked me to get three towels. I slipped on the tiles while she let the warm shower water flow over her body. I opened the shower door to find a crack. "Will you come out?" What beautiful, glowing, young skin she had as the water flowed over it. She stepped on the towel with which I had already dried myself. With a burst of laughter, she threw her arms around my neck and pressed tightly against me. "Now we're both wet again! We need three towels, maybe four!" and she laughed again.

I used one towel to dry her hair. "With the other one, you must go nice and firm over my body. That's what Hermann always does. I like that. What about your face and breasts?" I asked. "You understand what I mean," she said. I was assigned a pair of Hermann's pajamas, which were far too big for me. Gudrun also appeared to be wearing pajamas.

She suggested drinking coffee in the kitchen and eating a piece of the mocha cake she had made that afternoon. I was sent to close the curtains in the kitchen.

She asked me to sit in the same armchair as last time and put the cups and plates with a giant cake on the table next to it. She fetched the package I had brought her from the hall and sat on my lap. The handbag was approved, and I asked her to look at it. I had put a small box of chocolates in it, and a brooch was at the bottom. The BVD paid for everything, but they only knew about the bag. The thanks quickly turned into caresses and kisses. I ran my hands and fingertips over her soft, warm skin.

She got a nightgown. "How do you like this?" she asked. "Neat and solid, but you look cozier in those pajamas," I said. "Do you think so?" asked Gudrun with some doubt. I smiled. "You're kidding me!" she exclaimed. She grabbed a jar from the counter, and before I knew it, she was smearing a dollop of mocha cream on my face. She started licking me off. She remarked disapprovingly that I had beard stubble. The previous day, I had shaved, but all night and day, I had traveled and sat with Ebi and Heiner. "You can shave with Hermann's stuff, but first, I have to finish with you," she said. After she licked me clean, we went back to the bathroom. I smoothed myself with Hermann's shaving gear. When I returned to the kitchen, she had dabbed a few licks of the soft brown cream over her nipples. She looked at me with a grin and said, "Now, lick me off!" I didn't let myself be told that twice.

She urged me to devour my coffee and cake. "Then we can have fun afterward. We now have a whole night for the two of us, although I have to take care of Hermann later." The cake was delicious. It was, of course, made with great love. "Did you put a little maraschino in the cake batter? My mother always does that." She didn't know maraschino, so I promised to bring that with me next time.

In bed, Gudrun rested her head on my shoulder. We cuddled and whispered some more before falling asleep together. At one point, Gudrun rudely awakened me. "Hermann is here. We should greet him and prepare something for him." Sleepily, I followed her to the kitchen. "So, there are Eve and Adam." Hermann greeted us with a smile. She walked up to him and kissed her husband. "How beautiful you are in these clothes," he said, giving her a sweet pat on the buttocks.

"How is it here?" he asked. "Peter was brought to the square too late," Gudrun replied. She told me what had happened. "Peter told the driver I needed him more than those drunks from the Stasi." Hermann reacted with concern. "I agree with your priority, but did you say that to the driver, Peter?" he asked. "Oh, Hermann, I told that driver that there would be no good conversation with the Stasi duo and that I had to help that lady because otherwise she risked getting sick. And I asked if they wouldn't want to be here too early tomorrow morning ". Meanwhile, Gudrun had prepared a good stack of sandwiches for Hermann: a dish of cheese, one of sausage and cold cuts, and two cups of milk.

Hermann said he would sleep on the couch because Gudrun and I 'needed' the bed. He wanted to know what I liked about Gudrun. "I fell for her eyes, the nice expression on her face, and especially her spontaneity," I said honestly. "So not for her tits?" I replied that I hadn't seen them until she removed her sweater. "It was the enthusiasm with which she pulled me from the square, the laughter, the hiding on porches, and the kissing. All of that together did it for me."

"Has Gudrun ever told you?" Gudrun interrupted him. "I told him that last month." She enthroned me, walking backward, and held my hands. At the bed, she pulled me towards her, pushed me on, and fell on top of me. "So, now you can't leave!" She pulled the blankets over us. First, we are going to get nice and warm again."

Eberhard and Heiner arrived at the door at about eight o'clock the following day. Hermann opened the door and came to call us. He left the bedroom door ajar. Then he went to tell Ebi and Heiner that we were getting dressed. The announcement that they were there spurred Gudrun to engage in extra activity. She wanted something from me one more time. After our boisterous morning exercise ended, we went to wash and dress.

"We're going in together, you know," she said conspiratorially. "Then we'll have breakfast first." "That's my doctor's prescription," I replied. I explained to her that I had epilepsy and that, according to the doctor, I could have a seizure if I didn't have a full stomach. "I think you are completely normal and strong," said Gudrun. I agreed, but I said, "Last night, I took a pill in front of you, and I will do it again shortly."

Eberhard, of course, wanted to take me with him immediately, but Gudrun stood right before him. "You're not getting him yet. Peter has been seriously ill for many years. You overlook that because he regularly takes medication. He must also have a good breakfast first. For his morning pill and breakfast, you mustn't cause him any tension, either ". Ebi was perplexed. Hermann offered him and Heiner coffee. "You will need that after yesterday," he said. His remark turned out to be an effective means of silencing them.

After breakfast, there was nothing else to do but say a fond farewell to Gudrun and also warmly to Hermann. "I hope to see you again next month. Will you bring me something again?" Gudrun asked. Eberhard beat me to it. He firmly said he would make sure we never saw each other again. I promised Gudrun I would try to pass by again in the coming months with a little bottle of maraschino. But Eberhard stood so firm, as I had not seen him before and would not see him again. After a firm goodbye kiss and her cry, "I will always remember you," Ebi pushed me out of the apartment. Heiner closed the door behind us.

Heiner drove. Eberhard sat upside down next to him to talk to me. I let him go because I didn't feel like talking. I was still tired from all the talking and activities with Gudrun between sleeping. Ebi gave a monologue on morality in the relationship between husband and wife, saying that "people in a position like me couldn't afford to get involved with members of the opposite sex." When he more or less forced me to say something, too, I said, "Ah, Eberhard, ordinary people like those with whom I have now had such nice contact don't care about morals, politics, religion, or military matters. To talk. We are talking about work, love, school, family, your childhood life, your hobbies and sports."

That Sunday, I was ordered to buy a DSLR camera. That would allow me to photograph documents. It was tempting to ask my colleague and former photographer, De Wit, for advice. Both Ebi and the Deugniet duo urgently advised me against this. Ebi had given me a suggestion for a prize, and the BVD men inquired with their experts. The BVD also gave me a carefully measured advance.

I photographed the documents in daylight so as not to use a flash. That immediately worked well because I firmly attached the camera to the edge of my desk to make fine adjustments easily. Later, I had to buy more accessories for the camera, such as films of all kinds of speed and sensitivity, a telephoto lens, and a bag for all of those things. I was also instructed to obtain and photograph certain documents. It always turned out to be public documents you could copy in a library. I took pictures of those copies. I gave the copies and the photos to the BVD. I only got the photo film back with the comment that it was okay. After the first time, however, the BVD told me not to go to the library anymore. Then, there was a stamp from the library indicating that information was accessible to everyone. I was better off requesting original documents from, for example, the Ministry of Defense.

I resolved to say as little as possible to the BVD about my antics from those days in East Berlin. Of course, that didn't work. The gentlemen thought it was stupid that I had run away and even more ridiculous that

I had thrown a stone through a window. "You can count on your fingers that you will be arrested for that, right? It's in their best interest to get you out of trouble. You might say a little too much to the wrong police officer. You did not have a passport at that time. You hardly have a leg to stand on if you want to call in the help of the Dutch embassy. Stupid, stupid, stupid."

They listened open-mouthed when I asked the taxi driver to return and tell Ebi that Gudrun needed me. I also mentioned that I had added that talking to Ebi and Heiner that night was pointless because of their alcohol consumption.

"Most people, including spies, approach something like this more carefully, Peter," said Van der Niet. Like last time, they wanted to know all about what Gudrun and I had done. I told them that I had turned on the shower for Gudrun and advised her to go under it. I also mentioned that I gradually warmed up the water. I didn't say I went to stand with her. Van der Deugd, who appeared to be friendly, was interested in the mocha cake.

Afterward, I heard that my riots in East Berlin had led to much merriment at the BVD office.

7. Little Red Book Mao is not welcome

If you travel with frequent waiting or are bored during a plane or train journey, you can only sometimes study chess problems. A Western newspaper was forbidden to be read in Eastern Europe. So, for a change, I bought the Red Book of the Chinese leader Mao Zedong at the station in Utrecht. China was a communist country, and Mao preached a "Cultural Revolution" there.

Red booklet by Mao Ze Dong

In masses of hundreds of thousands, the Chinese marched through the cities, brandishing the booklet and uncritically chanting the theses and slogans of their leader. That booklet contained 427 pieces of it. I bought it for fun because I enjoyed reading the sentences and, in my eyes, mostly the nonsense in them. Mao dates back to the year 1893. In 1943, he became Chairman of the Communist Party of China. In 1954, he created the position of Chairman of the People's Republic of

China. Likely, he already had early dementia when he wrote down his thesis. Over the years, his mind got increasingly on the run with him. Still, no matter how much his body and mind weakened, he remained - partly due to the influence of his fourth solid wife, Jiang Qing—in power until his death on September 9, 1976.

Checkpoint Charlie (American Zone), western side

Because I had often heard about Checkpoint Charlie, I had asked Eberhard if I could also cross the border there. Berlin was then divided into a Russian (east), an American, a British, and a French zone. At Checkpoint Charlie, you went from the American to the Russian sector. The difference was that East German border guards stood on the Russian side and American ones on the Western side, with some West German assistants for possible language problems. Signs said in large letters that you were leaving the American safe zone and going to the Soviet zone.

I walked across the border, and on the eastern side, guards checked my passport and then my luggage. As customary in the GDR, a border officer found Mao's booklet and called in an officer. No, I was not allowed to import that booklet into the GDR. "Come with me," said the officer, who took me to an interrogation room. A colleague of his joined us. My passport was confiscated, but my bag contained everything except the booklet I had. They started asking what I was doing. That was difficult because I couldn't say I was delivering espionage material.

The officers kept asking questions. My answers gave them a suspicion. After a while, the last man left the room, adorned only by a picture of the East German flag on one wall and one of Lenin on another. The other border guard said:

"We have to confiscate that book."

Why?" I asked. "China and the GDR are both socialist countries, aren't they?"

...CHECKPOINT CHARLIE, eastern (Russian) side...

"There is a big difference," said the officer. A lengthy exposition followed on the differences between the excellent Marxist-Leninism led by Moscow and the heresy of the Chinese leader. He didn't have to convince me; in my eyes, Mao was a whopper anyway because of the nonsense he sold to the world with his Little Red Book. "Right," I said. "I understand that the booklet is not allowed into the GDR. But can I pick it up again if I go back tomorrow?"

The officer never seemed to have heard such a stupid question. "You have to leave today. You can only enter the GDR with a day pass if you do not have a visa. There is no weekend pass. Subversive reading must be destroyed. That is no different."

"When I return to the Netherlands, I will buy another book like this," I replied. "I laugh my ass off at the nonsensical things in it. What do we do now?"

"You will have to wait a while. My colleague is now calling other authorities."

The officer also left the room to check on his colleague. I was left without a book and company but with my bag of chess books and a game. A moment later, the officer came back in. "Hey, are you a chess player?" he asked. "Shall we play a game? We'll have to wait a while now. Someone will pick you up here."

The police officer took off his cap and got some coffee. I was a reasonably strong chess player then, but he was also good at it. We played chess for about an hour and a half before Eberhard arrived. When asked if I was coming along, the officer responded with the request that we "finish our party." As you know, meanwhile, "while" is an elastic concept. Eberhard had to wait another half hour and became increasingly impatient. In the end, we therefore decided to draw. I didn't get a day pass for Saturday at that time.

Ebi's car was around the corner. He was terrified that US border guards would recognize the vehicle as a spy car. His fear made no sense because the Americans had no watchtower at the border post. The East

Germans did, as with any above-ground border post. From those towers, all people and cars coming east were photographed.

In the car, I got my thunder, as expected. Why do you have to put on your elephant skin? Then Eberhard said, "We have lost precious hours because of this!" "You have plenty of hours if you repeat less and less and ruminate everything discussed like a cow," I growled.

Although we made up some of the lost time—approximately 150 minutes during the day—there was still not enough time to hand in my assignment, tell about my experiences with it, and talk about a new assignment. I did not fly back to Dusseldorf that Saturday but had to stay the night. It happened in the house I had been to, deep in East Berlin. On arrival, only one case of beer was too little for Heiner and Ebi's liking. The house lady had let us in and said that her husband was still shopping, so there wasn't enough bread yet. There were no supermarkets in those days. So, the man had to go to the nearest neighborhood grocery store by bike to get more beer, bread, cheese, and meat. However, grocers have always been extremely scarce in residential areas.

The mood that day could have been more pleasant. I can quickly get over differences of opinion. Ebi seemed to have more trouble with that. True, they repeated less than before, but whenever it seemed convenient, Ebi would scoff at me over my delays at the border. "You should know you're not allowed to take such a booklet."

Because I had to stay longer, the program for this weekend, at the end of June 1967, included sending "blank" letters (see chapter Paper, codes, and false passport).

The new assignment involved applying for accreditation at Accent, Central Europe's highly secret NATO headquarters in Brunssum (South Limburg, Netherlands). They wanted me to go to a press presentation there. I clarified that I had little or no interest in military affairs.

In the Netherlands, Van der Niet and Van der Deugd told me they were happy with this assignment. "Then we know that you're going there and not someone we don't know. We want to ask you to keep your eyes and ears open. If you think someone in the party could be a spy, you should be able to describe him as best you can for us," Van der Niet said. The "dads" enjoyed the story about the Little Red Book.

8. Off to the postal address

S hit! My East German and Dutch supervisors said I'd made a mess of things. I missed Eberhard in the brown, dirty, smelly Stasi pub. The train had been delayed for hours. It had been held up in the West, and as a result, when we arrived in the East, there was another inspection, and everyone was awakened. Due to that, I arrived at the pub on Hausvoigtplatz two hours late.

I find it difficult to grasp how a spy's supervisor can head off home when the spy he's managing doesn't appear at the agreed-upon time. As a critically thinking person, after a cup of coffee, I decided that I had two options: a) return home without achieving anything, or b) find Eberhard and make the trip successful.

I decided on the latter as somebody who attaches importance to time and money. I knew the address to which I'd sent the "blanco" letters. It was one of the most prominent streets in East Berlin: Karl-Marx-Allee 63. The Allee started at Alexanderplatz and went through to the Frankfurter Tower, where it changed its name to Frankfurter Allee. It was too broad, so building the underground Line 5 beneath it was easy.

From the pub, I had to walk a few miles. After three-quarters of an hour, I rang a doorbell. An older woman opened it. I told her I knew the address because I sometimes sent letters there. She was panicky! She called her husband, then shoved me into the front room and gave me a copy of the SED party newspaper, the communist Neues Deutschland

(New Germany). Furthermore, she then disappeared without saying a word.

The newspaper was bland, and I scanned it. The current Neues Deutschland is still gray, but since it's now published in a social democratic market economy, it has improved. Neues Deutschland was full of domestic-party propaganda. What little foreign news opinion and straight news it had were mixed. I learned in my journalism studies to separate these.

The woman of the house returned to give me a cup of tea. She kept her mouth firmly shut, but her offer of a cup of tea with milk and sugar was a sign of hospitality (although I didn't use milk). Meanwhile, I took out my chess game to pass the time.

Finally, after about half an hour, Eberhard appeared. It was noon. Mr. and Mrs. Anonymous waved to me from the door, and I thanked them again for the tea. Ebi talked of them as if they were dirt.

He was obviously in a bad mood. In the car, he told me it was very silly of me to go to people I didn't know and who didn't know me either. Now, the elderly couple had seen my face—the face of a spy. Then he told me I should not repeat such foolish adventures. I would have preferred to go straight home at that moment. The way Ebi insulted me got on my nerves, so I snapped, "You never gave me any instructions on what to do when I'm late or when we miss each other! I feel you didn't mind an extra-free day, but that's not how we will work together." We continued exchanging jibes but settled into a silent calm after a while. He looked out the window on his side and me on mine. He didn't say a word.

When we arrived at the villa, Heiner, who was already there, began again with the same old story. So I interrupted him and said, "If you intend to recite Psalm 119 to me, then I'll take out my chess book and game!" They were silent for a moment. Then, in unison, they said, "What is Psalm 119?" I wasn't surprised that atheists who believe religion is the opiate of the people didn't know this. I may have found it stupid, but I replied kindly, "Psalm 119 is the longest in the Old Testament, with well over a hundred verses." They were impressed by what they thought was my intimate knowledge of the Bible.

It was a signal to change the subject and get down to business. Because we'd lost four hours, I couldn't travel back on the day pass as I had intended.

"That is why we must find you somewhere to sleep," Eberhard said dryly.

"Well, I can think of one," I said hopefully.

"As Gudrun's? No, you must be fit tomorrow morning to forget that."

"As Gudrun's, I can switch off and sleep well without alcohol in my blood. It's different for you, with all your smoke and beer," I said in rebuttal. I wanted to spend time with this lovely woman. My thoughts drifted to her delicate body, soft, warm skin, and beautiful, shining brown hair. I could feel how she pressed my head against her wonderfully warm tummy while I stroked her breasts.

Heiner rudely awakened me from reverie. "Hey, we've got to work. We've wasted enough time—no more dreaming. What have you got for us?" he asked loudly in his fine, full voice, unlike Ebi, who sounded like a whistling, creaking cart pulled by a horse.

I dug into my bag for the rolled documents and the roll of film from the bottom. I wouldn't say I liked walking from the pub to Karl Marx Allee 63, but I genuinely looked forward to Ebi and Heiner's reaction. Before the call from Mr. Anonymous, they had been dealing with more pleasant issues. All I could do was ask myself what the "good-for-nothing duo" would make of this.

"Things worked out well again this time. You have a more profound understanding of what we want from you. This information is beneficial," Heiner said.

"Then you can pay me well for it," I said.

"Typical capitalist, not nice," Ebi said.

"We have a common business agreement. I deliver you the things you want, and you pay me. This must be a mutual relationship."

Don't we pay you well?" Ebi asked.

"That's a matter of opinion. We both know how much you pay me. I had to put significant effort into this. I know how much I can get for an article as a freelancer in the Netherlands. I'd get the same money and put in half the time there. That gave me a good reason to go to Karl Marx Allee 63. Time is money. If I'd gone home, you'd have had to pay me the standard fee and compensation for the extra time spent traveling because of you.

"I don't understand," Heiner said. "Wasn't it your fault that you were late?"

"It wasn't my fault that the train was late getting to Berlin. Because you left the pub, and we lost two hours. Because Eberhard only fetched me after another hour and a half, you and the train are to blame for my delay. We had discussed that I would arrive today. And Heiner, you also have to pay for travel time. The trip from the Netherlands on the night train doesn't cost me time because I have to sleep anyway, but I miss my weekly chess evenings.

If I leave here at midday, I get home at eight or nine o'clock in the evening—a whole working day. On a typical day, I make fifty Guilders;

on weekends, I make an extra fifty percent, which makes seventy-five. I would get travel money twice for this and the next trip."

Then things heated up and worsened because they were swimming in vodka and beer, and I had to eat bread with greasy sausages so the alcohol didn't go to my head. But I felt that Heiner understood quite well what I was getting at.

Back in the Netherlands, I discussed the events with the "good for nothing duo." I started Everything very factually. Van der Niet wrinkled his forehead the entire time, but both men laughed when I finished my story. "Peter," he said, "behind the Iron Curtain, individual initiative is impossible. If the Communist Party were to allow that, they'd quickly lose control over society. Even well-trained agents need help to cope with people who take the initiative. Besides, it's common in such a case for spies to return home empty-handed. Then you reschedule. You indeed have to be paid extra in such a case. They could have done this, especially since you had to stay another day. They probably expected the question.

MARGA FALLS FROM THE Clouds

The business part of our conversation went so smoothly that I suggested I fly back to Düsseldorf on Saturday in East Berlin instead of taking the train on the same day. I told Ebi and Heiner that I'd gotten to know a girl named Marga on a trip to Vienna, Budapest, and Prague in August. She expected to see me in the Netherlands that evening, so a flight partway made sense. I could apply my refund for the train ticket towards the plane ticket. The difference was insignificant, thanks to the federal government's subsidies for flights between Berlin and West German cities. To my surprise, Heiner and Ebi agreed. Ebi dropped me off early in the evening at the eastern entrance of Friedrichstrasse station, and I made my way to Tempelhof.

When I went to buy a ticket to Düsseldorf, I had bad luck: the best flight was already full. I had to wait an hour and a half, so I passed the time with chess. Arrival in Düsseldorf was delayed another twenty minutes, and it was too late to catch the last train to Amsterdam, so I had no choice but to seek a hotel close to the train station.

I had to let Marga know I wouldn't arrive that evening. At that time, she didn't have a telephone at home. Since the police claimed to be our best friend and helper, I called them in Haarlem and asked if an officer would be so kind as to tell Marga that I had missed the last train from Düsseldorf. Marga knew I worked regularly in Berlin but didn't think I went to East Berlin.

At the end of August, the BVD began to collect information about her and her family. They were also gathering information about her father's employer, the publishing house Spaarnestad. There were guys from the old school still working there, so my future father-in-law knew the same day that the BVD had obtained information about him and his daughter. Of course, as he mentioned at home,

Marga's sister, who was also on the trip when I met Marga, immediately assumed it had to do with her. She had encountered a stateless Greek in Prague who wanted to flee to the West. She had the idea to hide him in the bus's luggage compartment. Our tour guide, Douwe, nipped the project in the bud.

Marga had mentioned this to me a few weeks earlier after telling her I took orders for the BVD. The "Fathers," of course, had forbidden me from telling her because they wanted to say to her themselves "when the time was right." Van der Deugd did not say anything to her until June 1968, a month before our wedding, as she lay in the Maria Foundation Hospital with an inflamed appendix. To the BVD's amazement, she reacted theatrically, as we'd rehearsed, feigning surprise and scolding me for never telling her. To her family, Marga said nothing until long after the Berlin Wall fell in November 1989.

That September evening, when I was due to return from Berlin, Marga wondered where I was, and she was worried. She told me later that her parents would probably have panicked if I had told them. But her worries escalated almost to a panic when a police car pulled up out front. She quickly ran to the front door, which her father usually opened when he was home. The officer didn't even have to ring the bell, and before he could say anything, Marga asked, "Is something wrong with Peter?"

In a calm voice, he replied that her fiancé had called from Düsseldorf to let her know he'd missed the last train to Amsterdam and wouldn't arrive until the next day. She was relieved, as she was the following month when I proposed to her.

═══════════

During my meeting with the "good for nothing duo" a few days later, I casually asked how they would learn in the Netherlands if I was arrested in the GDR. "Frequently, we hear from relatives and the police when a double agent doesn't return when he's expected. Neither was suspicious of my question; they'd never been asked that. Marga's experience was not mentioned until 1970, at the farewell dinner in the restaurant De Biltse Hoek. The dinner was between the two men from the BVD, Marga and me, and the end of the spying.

═══════════

9. Laughter at the Dutch intelligence

In the following chapters, I'll discuss orders that I've gotten from Eberhard Molzan and his colleague, Heiner. Their instructions were usually idiotic. According to the BVD, neither of the experienced supervisors of West Europeans knew about the Western way of living and thinking. They needed to learn how to be the least noticeable in the West. Ebi and Heiner were, in my view, wholly nervous and didn't understand my saying, "Be normal, then you're mad enough," for not attracting attention.

In countries where the military and security services have essential government functions, people should avoid military installations and not take pictures. I was ordered to photograph the Soesterberg Air Base, the secret NATO AFCE NT headquarters in Brunssum, the headquarters of the Royal Air Force at Zeist, to name a few.

Shortly after the fall of the Berlin Wall and the elimination of the Iron Curtain between East and West, my wife and I got to know people in Prague, with whom we later became good friends. The first time they visited with us, we went on a tour of the Rotterdam port. By far the largest port in Europe, with all its bustle, it's much more enjoyable for foreigners than a canal cruise in Amsterdam.

We also sailed along the Rotterdam Dry-dock Company, where a submarine rested on the pier. The husband wanted to photograph the boat but thought it was prohibited, as he came from an East European country. He said, "This is a military object. You cannot take photographs, right?"

"Of course, you can," we replied. "You can shoot away at your leisure. No one will harass you later. A secret with a submarine is on the inside; one cannot photograph it."

When we took our tour, we didn't know that the submarine was no longer in service, but only for training purposes and to attract governmental customers. The Navy had all military parts wholly dismantled. That had been impossible with the torpedo tubes, but they were made unusable. Finally, during the 1990s, the submarine seal was sold as scrap metal.

Our Czech friend thought it was too risky to photograph the submarine. He felt the same way about the oil refineries of Shell and Esso. Like military installations, refineries and steel processing plants are, under dictatorships, considered strategic objects. What is produced in a steel factory, you can't tell from the outside. But with some general education on refining technology or refineries, you can identify the plants. The towers of a crude oil distillation plant are broad at the bottom and narrower at the top. The most important products of such a refinery are gasoline, diesel, kerosene, and naphtha. There are separate installations to convert surplus fuel oil and bitumen into profitable products.

If you use Google Earth to search for the North Korean capital of Pyongyang or the ancient Iranian city of Qom, with its nuclear facilities in the area, little is hidden today. Satellites send razor-sharp images of streets, buildings, and homes, showing the total built-up area in strict dictatorial cities.

At any rate, the BVD found two photo assignments that the East Germans had given me to be quite hilarious. Contrary to any warning from Eberhard and Heiner, I had photographed a guard in front of a building at the Headquarters of the Royal Air Force at Zeist. The next time, I was even in a photo myself. A photographer had photographed the American jets and had taken a picture of me and other photographers at the airbase in Soesterberg.

Of course, the BVD people knew that their counterparts on the other side of the Iron Curtain would react in horror to this. A totalitarian regime can't present itself this way. At the same time, this provides a good cover in the West.

The same was true for the story about when I took my then-fiancée to a meeting at NATO headquarters in Brussels. A French lieutenant colonel was flattered that a young lady at the dinner table unexpectedly accompanied him.

10. Marga and the French Kolonel

During the Cold War, the East Germans naturally wanted to know everything about NATO and the military intelligence services. Ebi and Heiner wanted me to get press credentials at AFCENT, one of three NATO operational-level commands (then Allied Joint Force Command [JFC] Brunssum, Netherlands). AFCENT was located in a former coal mine near Brunssum. It was an open secret that the military command was deep in underground shafts.

After France withdrew from NATO in 1966, AFCENT moved from Fontainebleau to Brunssum in 1967. In the event of war, the underground command center offered secure protection against a nuclear attack. According to rumors, gigantic amounts of food, water, and a disposal site were stored there. More precise information about this underground command center was and remains top secret.

Since 1977, after the period I spent as a spy, a large part of the activities there have been relocated to a gigantic bunker built into the landscape directly across the border in Germany. This large building has eight working and residential floors. The thickness of its walls is a secret.

After introducing myself, I received approval to go to AFCENT. But this did not mean that I was permitted to go underground. Now and again, all I could get was an invitation to a press conference in a former mine building above ground. However, I found nothing interesting about this. I could never muster the enthusiasm for military activities. Later, I became interested in other things: economics, agriculture, the geology of oil and gas fields, and nuclear technology. I'd always disliked weapons more complex than a simple catapult.

I never fulfilled my military obligation or learned to shoot. I once had a try at a fairground target range, but after two shots, the owner took the gun away from me even though I'd paid for three. Even with that rifle, I was a danger to other people.

However, after I visited AFCENT for the first time, the East Germans were as happy as little children. I only gave them reports, which were already public documents and had also been approved and probably copied by the BVD. There was nothing secret about their content.

Yet Ebi and Heiner reacted as if I'd fought a significant battle. They supervised several Dutch journalists from their offices, who were double agents. They always knew, for example, when there would be a press conference at NATO headquarters. Again, they ordered me off to NATO. Yet again, I had to go through the whole approval procedure for a press interview, yet it was approved.

I am curious to know how much the BVD was involved. The Fathers always denied it, but considering how fast my applications were approved, I assume I was helped somehow.

So, I went to the press conference at NATO headquarters in Brussels. One of my colleagues might have been a spy, and I concluded this from the way he asked questions and did not attract attention. Furthermore, I tried describing him to the BVD.

...NATO headquarters, Brussels...

As a journalist, I approached someone like this more directly, figuring he could provide me with additional information. When we met, I always introduced myself.

This trip to Brussels was on a weekend, and we were told to appear at the headquarters on Friday afternoon. Marga accompanied me on this trip; it was the only time I could take her with me. I got particular pleasure out of appearing there with my bride-to-be. Marga was also given a large writing pad and a pretty ballpoint pen from the North Atlantic Alliance.

After the journalists were welcomed in English and French, a French lieutenant colonel spoke, outlining the program. In this impressive conference room, nothing was left to chance. Interpreters translated speeches into each journalist's native language.

NATO also provided a fine hotel for guests. At half past seven that evening, we had dinner there, which was rather late for us Dutch. We'd devoured the snacks on the conference table to calm our rumbling stomachs. NATO was showing itself off at its best.

There was a seating plan for the meal. Marga, the spy's fiancée, was seated beside the French lieutenant colonel as a guest of honor. He was chivalrous, but he spoke only one language, his own. Marga had had four years of French lessons at school but no actual practice in the language. Fortunately, a Flemish journalist was sitting close to them, and he used his hands and feet to help with transiting. The lieutenant colonel enjoyed himself with the slim young woman by his side. That kept Marga relaxed.

I sat far away from her with the Dutch, Belgian, and German journalists. The Italians and Spaniards, who spoke only their native languages, sat with their colleagues.

We traveled back to the headquarters the following morning. Therefore, why NATO was so important was discussed in great detail. In forceful lectures, the speakers tried to convince us that the Warsaw Pact troops (Russia, its vassal states, and most East European countries) had supremacy in the air and on land. The navies of the East and West differed little, but taking everything together, the Russian arsenal was much more extensive.

"We can only make up this deficit," a young American officer said, "with more advanced weapons. We have fighter aircraft superior to the Russians and espionage aircraft flying at high altitudes, the famous U2s." The latter had undergone significant improvements since Lieutenant Colonel Gary Powers was shot down by a Russian missile in 1960. (That told the Americans that Russian missile technology had improved, but in violation of his orders, Powers did not destroy his U2 in the air and was taken captive.).

Now, they fly too high for Soviet fighters, and their missiles are not precise enough to be seen or followed in the air. (Search and destroy devices that react to heat; they did not exist then.).

"Our espionage aircraft have sensitive photographic equipment on board. In daylight, they can identify the movement of troops and materials. On the ground, and that is our greatest threat, the Warsaw Pact's supremacy is enormous. Western Europe is so small that they can launch a surprise attack and overrun us without deploying nuclear weapons. It is about 400 miles from the Iron Curtain to the Atlantic, while it is 1,800 miles from our border to the Urals," said an American general who attended the meeting on Saturday.

It was very recently (September 2013) that German newspapers published plans for a surprise and swift attack by East German and Russian troops on Western Europe. The newly discovered papers had yet to be analyzed in depth by the German Ministry of Defense.

It seemed as if NATO was between a rock and a hard place. One might ask if there was a political and humanitarian justification to deploy nuclear weapons first if the Warsaw Pact struck. Undoubtedly, the Russians would respond immediately.

One journalist asked, "You spy around so much; you must know where the Russians have located their nuclear weapons."

The general replied, "We assume we don't know all the locations. Russia is an enormous country with dense forests and mountain ranges, which are not easy for us to watch. We know that nuclear submarines are patrolling the American coasts as well as the coasts of Western Europe. We do the same. At the end of the Second World War, the Americans dropped two atomic bombs on Japan. The dreadful effects are all too well known. If America and Russia were to deploy their total atomic destructive capability today, America and Europe would no longer exist, and large parts of Asia would be destroyed. We reckon that, as a result of nuclear fallout, all life on earth would be endangered. It's realistic to assume that the planet will no longer be habitable for humans.

However, the Russians are also aware of this. We hope mutual fear prevents the White House and the Kremlin from pressing the red button. The terrible truth is that we must be equally armed to maintain a balance of power."

Journalists are usually always aware of words, but the room was quiet after this monologue. Perhaps because many couldn't write fast enough, this lecture's content and urgency made an impression because American officers always chose their words carefully and efficiently.

Before lunch, the journalists were allowed to speak to the military's top brass and Manlio Brosio, Secretary-General of NATO from 1964 to 1971. Journalists with military experience asked questions while I listened and took notes.

The event ended with a lunch. Afterward, Marga and I took a bus that dropped us off in the city center of Brussels, and we spent the rest of Saturday and part of Sunday exploring the city.

In East Berlin, the gentlemen were happy with all the photographed documents and my report on NATO. After the "Fathers" studied my report, they said they wouldn't be surprised if Ebi and Heiner would like the report as a photo. They recommended this if I wrote a detailed report on such a sensitive topic. I'd cut out an article from another newspaper about the press conference in Brussels and took it with the BVD's approval.

As long as they were so enraptured, it seemed ripe to ask for more money. "My cover is costing much money, and having my fiancée with me made it easier to ask for information," I argued.

The East Berlin duo agreed. I'd taken an essential step toward becoming a proper spy. They increased my fee by fifty West marks permission. I was not particularly impressed by the meager amount and ensured they got the message.

Van der Deugd and Van der Niet weren't surprised. They, too, saw I was making progress, so they said they'd raise my salary for subsequent months. But I also found their raise somewhat miserly. I said I'd given them the fifty West marks from the East Germans, worth more than the fifty Guilders I got from the BVD. They were making sure that I could spend only a little. I felt that I was being patronized, and I told them so.

11. "Lie Down in the Ditch"

I n the spring of 1968, I received an order from the East Germans to photograph the Royal Air Force headquarters in Zeist. Because I was born and raised there, I knew the way to the southern perimeter besides the castle in Zeist and the municipal sports ground where Patria and Jonathan played football.

The start of Cow Street was well asphalted, but that was worse on the second little street to the left. In the end, the closer I got to the farm of Van der Grift (his son Johan and I had been together at the primary school for boys of the Evangelical Brotherly Church. There, after about 300 meters, was the mansion The Wulperhorst (a 'wulp' is a rather large bird that lives in swamps and on beaches). The original mansion dates back to 1772, but after a fierce fire, it was rebuilt and modernized in 1858 in the current style. Behind the house is a vast and exceptional garden until the meandering old Curving Rhine. That is in particular because of the water management. That is regulated via several ditches for the discharge and supply of water from the Curving Rhine. As a result, the garden is a swampy area with its natural habitat. This was part of the landscape with a few other waterways and trees.

Mansion Wulperhorst

The house is now situated on a 12.5-acre nature reserve. It is part of Stichtse Lustwarande, a chain of over a hundred grounds and estates. A colleague of the architect had the house built for his two sons, Gijs and Hank. Hank died in 1950, after which the Ministry of Defense bought the building for the Air Force Staff. Later, it was used as a detention center for asylum seekers. In 1980, the estate was purchased by the Landscape Office of Utrecht, which let the house go to ruin. In 2001, concert pianist Wibi Soerjadi bought it. He dreamed of a piano academy, and for that, he needed space and tranquility. Since the house was utterly derelict, Soerjadi had to renovate it from scratch.

Ebi wanted me to take pictures of it. "Photographing a military headquarters is prohibited, so be careful not to get caught." He didn't know that in Western democracies, the outside of a building is not a secret, no matter how many secrets there are inside. "Make sure you take the photos from several angles because they want different perspectives."

When I stood in front of the building, to the left and right were a field and meadow belonging to the farmer. On either side of De Wulperhorst stood an odd bush or tree. Standing there, I should be on military property and thus liable to prosecution. The rear was impenetrable because of a marshy jungle, so I had no choice but to take the photos from the front.

I told Ebi this. "Are there guards?" he asked. I said there were.

"Could you hide behind a tree?" I had to laugh. "If three or four trees stand beside each other, then yes. These trees are quite young and have little room to grow between the path and the ditch," I said.

Ebi's face relaxed. "O, there's a ditch? Then, you have no choice but to lie down on the edge of the ditch and take pictures from there. The guard won't realize what you're doing," he said.

"I doubt that's a good idea. Doing that will attract his attention and make me conspicuous."

Ebi said, "Yes, but the guard should not see you taking a photo of the villa."

"You gave me the money for a good camera, so trust me to get you good photos."

"Just make sure the guards don't see you," Ebi said.

I decided continuing the conversation was useless, so I agreed, figuring I'd manage. And that's what I eventually did.

In the summer of 1968, during a lunch break and bathed in bright sunshine, I got on my bicycle with my camera around my neck, up to a series of mansions. They were once the reason Zeist was called 'the pleasure garden for the rich.' I rode past five such estates to photograph them before I set off to Wulperhorst. On arrival, I asked the guard if I could take a picture of the mansion from the road. I told him truthfully that I was taking photos of the mansions around Zeist for my collection. He permitted me, then retreated stiffly to a spot in front of his guardhouse. Naturally, I photographed him and the guardhouse, too.

When they saw it, the Fathers couldn't stop laughing at the photo of Wulperhorst, the soldier standing in front, exemplifying the Dutch way of discipline, not to be confused with German or American discipline.

Van der Deugd slapped his thigh as he said, "What a beautiful photo!" And I'm sure he meant something other than the technical quality.

"With ideas like that, you're slowly turning into a real spy," Van der Deugd said.

At a certain point, I returned to East Berlin. Taking the shortest route, I handed the roll of film over on a Saturday morning. Ebi and I went to the villa in the East we'd used before, and Heiner took the film roll with him to the Ministry for State Security. Around midday, he returned with the photos. Without saying a word, he handed Ebi the pile of developed prints. "Look what he did; he ignored all of our warnings."

Eberhard looked at the photograph lying on top of the pile. His face went tight. "Was the guard able to see you?"

"Yes, we even spoke friendly. I asked him if I could take photos of De Wulperhorst."

"That means he saw your face and would recognize you again," Ebi said.

"Ebi, Heiner, you don't know how life works in the West. As a journalist, I can work better in the open. If I'd hit upon the crazy idea of hiding behind a tree-lined path in a castle moat, the guard would have immediately become suspicious," I said.

"You're saying that in the Netherlands, you can simply take photographs of a military headquarters?" Ebi asked.

"Yes, I can, but you can't. I know what I can and can't say to a guard to get his permission. To get permission from a general, you need other arguments. As you can see, I took several photos of De Wulperhorst, one without the guard. From the technical perspective, it isn't such a great photo."

Heiner said, "Don't think you must give us security lessons. We're specialists in that."

"Heiner, how often have you been in a West European country since 1945?" I asked. "When I was fourteen, I wrote for my father's newspaper. From that moment on, I learned that a journalist always asks questions. This puts everyone on a pedestal, and they feel honored and are more inclined to be helpful, as was the soldier when I asked to take a picture. People are vain. In almost every case, you get what you want provided, and you stick to what's feasible."

He and Ebi admitted they'd never been to Western Europe. "But we supervise several West European agents. None of them has ever gone to the extremes you've gone to," Heiner said.

"Be cheeky enough, and you can get whatever you want," I said, but this and other Dutch expressions went over their heads.

I had an amusing conversation with the Fathers when I reported to them about handing over the photos of De Wulperhorst. "Yes, we knew how they'd react," Van der Deugd said.

12. Among the "Spotters"

The East Germans were interested in the air base at Soesterberg, where an American squadron was based. Their main interest was in aircraft, which I was ordered to photograph. Fighters had to be in the air constantly in case of intrusions into western airspace by Warsaw Pact aircraft. Should this occur, they would either be escorted back to the border or forced to land.

On weekends, mainly when the weather was good, hundreds of people always stood at the runway's end at Soesterberg to watch F4 Phantoms take off. It was an imposing sight. During the week, far fewer curious observers or spotters had already made the rounds of bases to photograph as many aircraft as possible. It was a competition, and the winner was the person who'd taken the most photos of aircraft on which the registration numbers could be read.

Heiner and Eberhardt asked whether I was allowed onto the base with a camera. I found the question stupid. First, it wasn't permitted, and second, the aircraft were usually in hangars, with three extra bases in Holland, apart from Soesterberg.

As editors of local newspapers, we naturally received invitations to festivities at the base. We were escorted from the gate to the hall on such occasions, where press conferences and awards ceremonies were held.

I'd already had a few enjoyable experiences there. The first was the return of Queen Juliana and her husband, Prince Bernhard, after a long trip abroad. On that occasion, I introduced myself and asked the prince a question. At our subsequent encounter, the prince was again available to the press, as his daughter, Princess Irene, and her boyfriend at the time, Carlos Hugo de Bourbon-Parma (formerly the Count of Parma), slipped out of the government aircraft unnoticed.

I brought again a question to Prince Bernhard, and despite meeting thousands of people each year, he remembered my name. Subsequently, I was able to speak to him in private.

Ebi and Heiner had asked me many questions about the base in Berlin. Can I take photos of it? My reply irritated them. "Is that not allowed here? Isn't it strange that you ask me to do this for you in my homeland?"

"That's why you were recruited," Heiner said and blabbered on with his questions about the base. They wanted photographs of the entrance gates at Dolderseweg and some of the end of the runway at Van Weerden Poelmanweg.

Heiner asked if I could take more photos through the bushes around the base. There were many bushes, but armed guards with dogs patrolled the perimeter regularly. From the corner of Dolderseweg, I couldn't reach the bushes because of buildings. "You can forget the bushes. I won't do that. I'd only arouse suspicion. I'm not sure if I can get to the entrance gates. I can try, but anyway, I'll be able to get the photos." (These could be found in any regional bookstore, but I didn't tell them.)

I ended the conversation on a hopeful note. "Eberhard, if you could give me money for a good zoom lens, I could probably take good photos of the whole base from Van Weerden Poelmanweg at the end of the runway." As usual, money seemed fine for East German intelligence if it allowed them to obtain photographs. Thus, I got the zoom lens. Once more, the BVD paid for this with the East Germans' West marks. But as far as my fees were concerned, it was a different story.

I first tried the zoom lens from the top of our apartment building in Zeist, eleven floors up. Then, on a good day, when I had a little spare time, I went with the camera to the end of the runway at Van Weerden Poelmanweg. I knew there were flights; I could hear and see them from home.

In the late morning, a group of about thirty curious spotters was already seated at the end of the runway, trying to identify the aircraft's registration numbers. This required high-speed film to freeze their movement since the plane had already reached speeds of some 180 mph when taking off.

When you heard a jet start off, you had to count off a second or so to lead the plane, anticipating when it would appear in the frame when you made the exposure.

... A Phantom from Airbase Soesterberg... (background removed)

The spotters were drinking beer, cola, and coffee, but fortunately, none were smoking. A snack van on the other side of the street was nearby for food. I noticed the crowd had broken into smaller groups of five to seven people.

I was warmly welcomed by one of these groups. As a newcomer, I quickly got the order to go to the van and fetch food. They also asked me to show them my camera and tell me a little about myself. Of course, I told them I worked for the newspaper in Zeist, and their photographer developed the film for me. That was the cue for the others to start discussing developing techniques. The spotters, incidentally, have yet to learn about my adventures as a spy.

The spotters did give me tips on how to photograph jets. They taught me the best angle to hold the camera, how to preset the distance, and when to open the shutter. Jets fly so fast that you must press the button before you see them in the viewfinder, a real challenge! According to some of them, this was different at Amsterdam airport. There, it was a matter of releasing the shutter when the plane was at an angle of forty-five degrees on the runway, slow enough for photographing.

After I'd taken a few photos, one of the guys asked me to go for a walk with him. We walked over the slight rise beside the road, which led almost directly to the runway. "Give me your camera, and I'll take a photo of you," he said. Then, he waited until a jet took off with a thunderous roar. As I looked at the runway, I could see the aircraft approaching. My friend opened the shutter just as the pilot ignited the afterburners. "Now you've got a photo for your scrapbook," he said proudly. When the photo was printed, the enormous flame was visible in the shot, as were some other observers.

From where I was standing, I took more photos of the runway, the observers, the snack van, and a few people standing at the fence. Two pictures of the fighters were so good that the registration numbers were precise.

I also asked the BVD to develop excellent and poor photos so I could later show them to my fellow spotters. They, of course, had numerous comments.

The photos of the runway, me, and the observers on the other side of the road ranged from passable to sound. Still, through the opportunity at the air base, I discovered a joy in photography. I went back to the same place a few times to take photos. The crowd of spotters changed.

The Fathers had fun with the photos—especially the ones of me and the observers. I presume they photographed the pictures. One of me was on the roll of film as I returned to the group with my hands full of croquettes and fries. I never found out who'd taken the photo with my camera, but the BVD had a good laugh over the image of the spy. They already knew what the reaction would be in East Berlin.

Ebi and Heiner turned pale in the East Berlin villa when they saw the photos. They gazed at the pictures of me with the French fries and croquettes, one of the lit afterburner, and one of the people with cameras. "You were among all those people?" Ebi asked incredulously.

He held some photos up and said, "This is bad. Western intelligence agents could have sat there trying to expose spies."

I poured oil on the fire. "Yes, Eberhard," I said, "I was sitting right in the middle. I gave them my name, where I work, and everything else."

Eberhard moaned. Heiner couldn't think of anything to say. "Peter, Peter, Peter," Ebi cried. "For your safety, I advised you last time to lie in the ditch and never let yourself be photographed. I tried to stress the importance of following security instructions."

I interrupted him. "If I did that, I'd be exposed immediately as a spy. I have enough experience to judge. A Dutch says, 'Behave normally, then you're crazy enough.' If I behave normally in my surroundings," Eberhard waved his hand to interrupt, but that just made me press on with more voice volume. ". If I behave normally, I go unnoticed. If I take your advice, I will show myself as a spy. I have no desire to do that, and you gain nothing if I do. I have no idea where you get your wisdom from, but your organization seems pathologically disturbed."

That wouldn't be a compliment to Markus Wolf, the big man from the General Reconnaissance Administration, who, like many other communists, was more married to his work than to his wife.

My condemnation momentarily rendered Ebi and Heiner speechless, but the silence didn't last long. As spies' handlers always think they're right, it was the same story with the fathers. Ebi and Heiner never admitted that they lived in a totalitarian regime and that their definition of democracy scoffed at all Greek wisdom in this domain.

In their "democracy," a party ruled, and within this party, there were associations called parties. In these associations, you can find professional groups and cooperatives. In this way, the People's Chamber reflected the population, but all with the same ideological convictions. Resolutions were adopted by the Central Committee of the Socialist Unity Party of Germany without any opposition from the People's Chamber.

Ebi and Heiner did not share my opinion. I let them think they had convinced me because I feared an endless lecture on security. I'd listened to that rubbish the previous time I had to photograph the headquarters Zeist (see previous chapter). By this point, I had decided to go my own way.

13. NATO Exercises Red vs. Blue

In September 1968, I received the order from East Berlin on short notice to go to NATO maneuvers in Denmark. I wasn't happy because Marga and I had just been married and wanted to have our first child as soon as possible. The BVD understood that now that I was married, I wanted to focus on my wife and eventual child.

In East Berlin, on the occasion of our meeting, they took a different view. "But don't you say business before pleasure?" Ebi asked. I was surprised he knew a Western saying.

"Yes, we say," I replied, "but you misunderstand the meaning. I work at the newspaper. My work for you is part-time, and family matters shouldn't be second place. You can't compare this spying to my real job, which, in any case, doesn't take me out of town."

Now, Eberhard brought his big guns to bear. "Once you're finished learning, you can earn a good salary with us. Then you no longer need your father's newspaper."

"Eberhard," I said, "then I would never be able to reveal the source of my income. I need a legitimate income to ensure a black income doesn't appear in my taxes."

"In that case," he replied, "we can give you the necessary instructions. If you were to buy a little house in a quiet corner of the Netherlands, where nobody knows you, the expenses are low. For the tax office, we will think of something."

"I borrowed money from my aunt to furnish our house. What would I buy a house with?"

"Peter, don't worry. You're still learning, which will take a little longer."

"Then let's talk about the job you've done for me. Going to the NATO maneuvers will take much extra time, for which I must be well paid."

Eberhard and Heiner looked at each other. They hadn't expected this. I set a high price because I'd have to take a week's holiday to attend the exercise. I had a few holidays left because of our honeymoon. If I could have gone to the maneuvers as a journalist, it wouldn't have been a problem. I had to ask my Dutch boss for days off without explaining why. I'd make the trip only if I received a hefty bonus on top of the standard fee.

Ebi and Heiner were now thoughtful. "How much do you think of?" Eberhard asked.

"Right, I now get permission for 250 marks," I said, "which is work I can do on my time off. You want me to take a week off; you must pay 250 to 300 marks extra for a whole week."

They could only decide by consulting a higher authority, they said. I said I wanted to know before I started. I had their backs to the wall. Heiner said he needed advice and went out the door. It didn't take long; he probably called someone. When he returned, he said a definitive answer wasn't possible this Saturday. Still, he was told that the answer would come via a secret radio message.

"Do I understand correctly what will be in a coded report, whether you accept my request or whether you do not accept it?" I asked.

Is it a requirement, Peter?" Ebi asked.

"Yes, I want a clear yes or no next week."

"You know, 250 marks is much money."

"I get more than 250 for a week's work. I said 250 to 300 marks extra, but I considered 300."

"But your boss also pays you for your vacation, right?" Ebi asked.

"It's not a vacation for me," I replied. "For those days off, my boss doesn't pay me wages. And they're not holidays for my wife. She's sitting home alone while I go off to work for you. For this, I require 250 marks for the job, plus a minimum of 250 marks extra for the week and money for expenses."

"That's a lot," Ebi said.

"If you say no, I won't do it. And I need to know soon, as I have to apply for vacation time, organize everything to be at the maneuvers, and apply for approval."

My employer paid me for this week. However, I was broke after our honeymoon and wanted to earn a little extra.

A week later, I heard they agreed to my terms on the radio. After my weekend visits to Berlin, I usually met the BVD people on Monday or Tuesday. When I returned this time on a Monday evening and received a phone call from The Hague, I asked to move the date to the end of the week. I wanted to wait to hear from Berlin. I was vague, but the BVD guessed it had something to do with a radio report.

This time, for once, the radio reception was good. I had been taught to decode messages from East Berlin and had the money to buy a transmitter. The messages from East Berlin were on different wavelengths, all on a very short wave. Sometimes, they were so close that it was hard for me to pick the right one for a particular night. The next day was always on a different wavelength.

Of course, Van der Deugd and Van der Niet wanted to know what the "yes" from the East Germans meant, as I had told the BVD in advance, and they had a copy for the decoding. They also wanted to know everything about the new job. They were curious about the East Germans' reaction to what I had delivered. I wished Van der Niet had not been present for this interview. He thought it would be great if I got an extra 250 marks. "But don't think you'll get the same from us. From us, you get a monthly allowance, while the East Germans pay you per job."

I disagreed, and now I must also haggle with the BVD. "Listen," I said, "I cannot put in extra time, money, and effort to comply with an order only to have the extra money I get to go to the BVD. Since my boss doesn't pay me for this week, you have to."

Van der Niet replied, "That's not what we agreed to; we agreed on a monthly fee."

"I know," I said, "but when I put in much overtime for my intelligence chief, he benefits from it. So, hean also pay me a little more."

"A little, maybe, but not 250 guilders," Van der Niet said.

"All or nothing. Either the 250 guilders and you'll get back more than 250 marks in return, or I'll refuse the job, which will disappoint the East Germans."

"How will you justify that on your next visit to East Berlin?" Van der Niet asked.

"I won't because I just won't go anymore. I'll see you both once more to turn in my spy equipment, and that's the end of the story. Since I was always 100 percent loyal, you can't do anything to me."

I was now thoroughly enjoying myself and thought, Go for it! The BVD changed their position, but the negotiations with Van der Niet and Van der Deugd were more tedious than with Ebi and Heiner. As a Westerner, I had a clear advantage in negotiations over the East Germans. The fathers were also Dutch, so they had more experience.

"You said you're willing to pay me more," I said. "How much?"

Van der Niet said, "Fifty guilders."

"Not acceptable."

"What about fifty guilders for your wife because she has to do without you for a whole week and a hundred for you?" Van der Deugd suggested

"You negotiate with famed Dutch stinginess," I replied.

After further excuses, Van der Deugd said, "Peter, we'll offer you 200 guilders, and we do not want to discuss it further."

I'd gotten what I wanted. An expert probably would have gotten more, but I was pleased with the result as an amateur.

I already had the press credentials for the NATO headquarters in Brussels, so I asked if I could get one for the fall maneuvers in Denmark. It was simple enough. All I had to do was call them and send a copy of my ID, which gave me my profession. Again, NATO was very accommodating. I'd have to bear the cost of the railway ticket to Copenhagen, but they would cover accommodations, food, and beverages.

During the maneuvers, I spent time with other journalists in bumpy military buses that carried us across the training area. Over the bus's loudspeakers, we heard comments like, "Shit, we're hit." We laughed. "Have we been hit, too?" shouted one of the journalists. "No, we're invisible," the lieutenant accompanying us said with a grin. (Today, they'd say "stealth.") "A blue tank has been hit," the driver said over the loudspeaker. "Well," the lieutenant said, " the red side discovered its position. Nothing was hit because, in exercises, you don't destroy your equipment."

Hey, I thought a Blue tank had been hit. Ebi had told me that NATO always used blue and red to identify combatants in war exercises. In his opinion, blue always won because the Red Army and other Warsaw Pact armies recognized Red. I wondered how the Warsaw Pact played its war games. Eberhard said it was probably much like NATO, but he didn't know. "So, does the Red side usually win over the Blue?" I asked. He had no answer.

At the final press conference on the NATO maneuvers, a few generals with colorful decorations sat at a table. I dared to ask a few questions. Surrounded by the military and the journalists experienced in military matters, this required much courage.

I asked, "Why do the participants have the colors blue and red? Is blue associated with the Blue of NATO and the Warsaw Pact associated with red?"

"No, no," replied a general, "you just have to be able to keep the two groups apart. You can call them blue and red or robins and magpies." Laughter reverberated in the hall.

"Who won this time?"

The general grinned. "NATO Blue."

"Can you tell how the victory came about? During the maneuvers, land, air, and naval forces?"

The general said, "At sea, Blue was much better. As a Dutchman, you'll appreciate that your Royal Navy was assigned to the Blue. In the air, Blue was good, especially because of its missiles. But on land, the sides were equal."

Another journalist asked, "Were nuclear weapons used?"

"That makes no sense," replied the general. "We know that nuclear weapons lead to destruction. If Red presses the button, Blue reacts within a minute. There is no possible defense against this destructive force. We hope that mutual deterrence will prevent a war, which is why in these exercises, not even small nuclear weapons are used, as they, in turn, would force the enemy to use larger ones."

After the press conference, I wrote a report for a small press agency, which gave me twenty-five guilders. The more extended version went to the BVD and East German security. I also had photos of generals in full gear, provided by NATO, and some military equipment. With a detour along the BVD, I gave these things to the East Germans in a bag I'd received from NATO. Van der Deugd had suggested that with a grin.

Both services kept their word about the one-time bonus. The men in The Hague warned me to be extra careful with my spending because the extra income shouldn't attract attention.

14. Warsaw Pact Invades Czechoslovakia

Since I was a little boy in the boys' school of the Evangelical Brotherly Church in Zeist, to whom I have felt sympathy since then, this religion has originated in Moravia in the southeast of the Czech Republic. The founder was Jan Hus, who opposed the omnipotence of the Roman Catholic Church and was burned at the stake for heresy in 1415. As all protestants, they were persecuted throughout the centuries. Their first stronghold was the Czech city of Tábor, but they were driven out in the pope's name and moved in small groups throughout Central Europe. Some settled on the Duke of Zinzendorf estate, some miles east of Dresden. They called the village they built there Herrnhut: "under the protection of God."

Zinzendorf visited the Netherlands in 1732 with his friend Cornelis Schellinger, the master of Zeist. For the safety of people from the Herrnhutters society, he asked Schellinger to offer them some land. He could settle at two squares along the road to the Castle of Zeist. There, they constructed a Brother square and a Sister square. The church they built in 1768 is still used for all their religious observances. The inside of the church is very modest and white. In this community, people believe from the heart and in peace. This was also practiced in schools and by missionaries, especially in Suriname.

I repeatedly had to write reports and articles for the East Germans. I also took piles of documents and photos with me. I wanted to take the initiative and make a documentary about Herrnhut and church life there. To my great surprise, both the BVD and East Berlin granted permission.

I contacted the Brotherly Community in Zeist.

They thought it was great that I wanted to visit the brothers and sisters in Herrnhut. They offered wholesome cooperation and gave me books, letters, and photographs to take to that community. The brothers and sisters were informed of my forthcoming arrival and were asked to help me.

Eberhard insisted that I travel via Berlin. Earlier, I'd said that I wanted to call on Käthe. This was not well received. When I asked Käthe behind Ebi's back if it would be okay for me to visit her before or after my visit to Herrnhut, her response was negative; she was too busy. I feared that she'd been told to say so by a higher authority. Today, she can't remember.

I met Ebi in East Berlin while changing trains for Görlitz. I received more instructions from him, superseding others, that I should go to the police station upon arrival. I followed his instructions this time, and they were already aware of my arrival. In Görlitz, someone from the Brotherly Community picked me up at the station.

There was much activity in their community house that evening. I recounted a lot about the community in Zeist and life in the Netherlands. In addition, I also had a box with letters, photos, photo albums, and a few books about the Community in Zeist; all I left with them. The box had been examined at the border by both a guard and Ebi, who pretended to be looking for smuggled goods. This was how I got through customs with the little box so quickly.

Of course, the Herrnhutters asked me how I had managed to get everything through customs. I said, "I'd inform customs by letter in advance what I was carrying and who it was for."

I slept in the guesthouse, and the pastor joined me for breakfast, where I was treated with the utmost hospitality. We prayed together (he in German and me in Dutch) and casually conversed as we ate. The man was very open, and to my astonishment, all my conversations in Herrnhut were like this. When I asked about this, one of the people I met said, "Oh, here, we have no secrets for each other. We don't get involved in politics or ideology." I spent the second day interviewing and writing my report for Dad's newspaper at Zeist. The people at Herrnhut gave me many letters and documents for the brothers in Zeist.

The driver who'd collected me from Görlitz on the first day was to bring me back on the third day. Since we didn't have to be at the station until midday, he asked me if I wanted to see the East German army's camp area at the time of the Warsaw Pact's invasion of Czechoslovakia, which took place on the night of August 20–21, 1968.

Brezhnev, the Russian party chief, disagreed with the course of the Czechoslovakian communist party or the government. Under Alexander Dubcek's leadership, they had supposedly deviated too far from the only acceptable Marxist-Leninist doctrine, the Russian version.

Alexander Dubcek

On January 5, 1968, Dubcek replaced the ultraconservative Novotny as head of the party. Novotny had always followed Brezhnev faithfully, which gave birth to the allegation that his policies had brought Czechoslovakia to the brink of economic ruin. Dubček advocated more liberal economic, scientific, cultural, and political liberties.

The latter two conflicted with Russian "ideology." It conflicted with the Russian aim of keeping control over the controlled states in Eastern Europe. Dubcek's aim wasn't to fight oppression. Still, within a short period, this led to increased political awareness, cultural life among the people, and economic improvement.

On May 4, Dubček was called to Moscow, where Brezhnev cautioned him to keep reforms within acceptable limits. Dubček refused to change his political style. In the months that followed, Moscow's threats became more intense. As censorship in Czechoslovakia eased, a public anti-Soviet stance developed, which Moscow would not tolerate.

Troops from Russia, Poland, Hungary, and Bulgaria were involved in the invasion. The GDR had troops ready at the border near Großhennersdorf. The East German leadership feared an uprising in their country if it became known that East German troops would help quell a revolution. From East German whispering, everyone knew there was no revolution in progress in Czechoslovakia but that Dubček sought to create a humane socialism.

Brezhnev was out of his mind with the fear of losing power, so he decided to invade after making sure the US wouldn't take this opportunity to attack Russia or other satellite states.

The East German troops camped in a pasture at the edge of a forest, where they went into hiding. When I arrived eight months after the invasion, everything had been cleaned up nicely. Not even a cigarette butt was to be found.

The BVD was surprised I'd seen the abandoned pasture where the East German army had been encamped. The Fathers asked a hundred questions, but I could only answer a few. They had to be satisfied with my best possible description and a map of the Free State of Saxony, where I could point out the location of this pasture. Herrnhut (five thousand inhabitants) was shown on the map, but Großhennersdorf was not.

The BVD was also surprised at how easily I managed to get letters, photo albums, and books out of the Brotherly Community in Zeist to Herrnhut. I sensed some skepticism in their questions. Fortunately, I could explain everything with the photographs, letters, and documents. Here, my camera was handy.

... Russian tank Prague 1968; the rude behavior by Russians is the reason people in Eastern Europe don't want them back...

The first target of the Russians was Radio Prague, which they destroyed. Still, the station kept broadcasting with a secret transmitter, which the Russians had installed at some point. They needed a week to find its location and silence it. Censorship was reintroduced, and Dubček was chased into a forest; he was relieved of his position as Communist Party secretary and joined the technical staff of the Slovak State Forestry Administration. After the fall of the Iron Curtain at the end of December 1989, he became president of the first free Czechoslovak Parliament. He died in 1992 as a result of a dubious car accident.

15. Papers, Codes, and False IDs

It's the nature of things that espionage requires communication between the intelligence service and the spy, for example, when a spy can't deliver on his mission by the deadline. It was not impossible to telephone or send telegrams to the GDR, but the Post Office first had to create a connection for all calls.

To the BVD's wiretapping line. Calls were also tapped in the GDR. At the time, personal computers and the Internet didn't exist.

My means of contact with the BVD was simple: I called a phone number in The Hague and stated my first name but nothing else. The switchboard operator then connected me with whomever I wanted to speak to. Such conversations were always kept short. For example, I would say, "I cannot be at the agreed time and place tomorrow. Can we meet two hours earlier or later?" The matter was dealt with in less than twenty seconds.

We also communicated in person in cars or restaurants. In a restaurant, for instance, we would agree to meet at half past two, but not at lunchtime. After lunchtime, we could sit safely from the others and avoid the risk of eavesdropping!

At the end of June 1967, I was given a pad with special paper and envelopes to communicate with East Berlin. To inform my GDR comrades of anything, I sent a letter to a man living at Karl-Marx Allee 63 in Berlin. Because of the address, residents knew they had to inform

State Security about a letter from the West. Then they would collect the letter.

The envelope contained just blank paper. A blank sheet whacked each of the pad's lined pages. I had to put cardboard under the blank one and write my message on the lined text with a ballpoint pen. Ebi told me to burn the lined piece of paper. For simplicity's sake, I gave it to the BVD in an open envelope and on blank paper. I got it back later, stuck a postage stamp, and mailed it. I had to take the letter to the post office at least two weeks before planning a meeting, and delivery and censorship took five to eight days.

I found it strange to send an empty sheet of paper. Why should the East German inspectors not become suspicious? Who would not know, if not the Western inspectors, that such a letter demanded more scrutiny? The name "Peter" and a post office stamp from Zeist were the only ways to identify me, but that was sufficient for them to find me at some point. For that reason, after sending a few empty pages, I wrote a chess letter and folded the blank sheet inside it.

The "Fathers" agreed with Eberhard and Heiner that it was a clever idea. I wonder if they'd ever recommended it to others. However, after the enthusiasm had waned, I told both parties that nothing should stand in the way of a pay raise because of my ingenuity. Writing chess letters took longer, but it was all right because they usually consisted of text from letters I'd received from friends.

I did receive more pay. Still, neither the BVD nor the East Germans used good performance as an argument. They have yet to mention my idea of the chess letters.

CODED MESSAGES VIA Radio

In early 1968, my East German companions told me they wanted to send me reports via short and ultra-shortwave radio. I was given training on a Saturday afternoon. By the end of it, I was utterly exhausted from all the endless repetitions. I wanted to feel cozy and go to see Gudrun. But, no—that wasn't allowed.

Nothing was spectacular about the code reports the Ministry for State Security sent me. Sometimes, codes were sent all day, but for me, only late in the evening on certain days. A monotonous female voice read out blocks of five figures, one after another. From the first block, I had to discern if the report was meant for me, and at the end was a final code with five figures. I had to memorize my personal recognition code at the beginning of the broadcast. For example, if my code was 54721, I had to be able to recognize it. Then the report could continue, for example, with 39246, a short pause, 85017, and the conclusion might be 11799. All the code blocks were on a code list they gave me, which I copied for the BVD. Decoding a report was a child's play. In this example, the word could have been "yes." The numbers were spoken clearly, yet I needed help initially.

I signed a note when given an advance to buy a radio. With the advance payment, I also got the information about the radio frequency and the days I should listen, as well as a set of codes. The paper showed that I contacted the GDR State authorities and received the codes for radio communication.

Eberhardt and Heiner thought I could be blackmailed after signing the certificate. They felt that now they had power over me in case I wanted to quit being a spy. In that case, copies of the note would be sent to my employer and police in the Netherlands.

I got bored listening to the emotionless female voice read out block after block of numbers without drawing a breath. On an adjacent frequency, called something like fishery frequency, you could hear the same. Even the voice sounded the same. Perhaps it was.

The frequencies for messages changed from day to day. First, I had to buy a radio. Then, I drew lines at the corresponding frequencies. I needed to improve with technology, so I bought a simple radio. The frequencies were so close together that I had trouble setting them correctly. Often, things went wrong, but fortunately, in this case, I wasn't alone. Specialists from the BVD were listening, but Ebi and Heiner didn't know. When I missed a few reports and the contents were necessary, the BVD helped me.

In East Berlin, they also noticed that each report was repeated twice on another day because I missed a radio report relatively often. I was rewarded for my stupidity with grumbling and sighs and another round of training. The problem was that I couldn't take the radio to East Berlin so they could show me what to do. It would have been confiscated as smuggled goods at the border. Meanwhile, the BVD refused to train me.

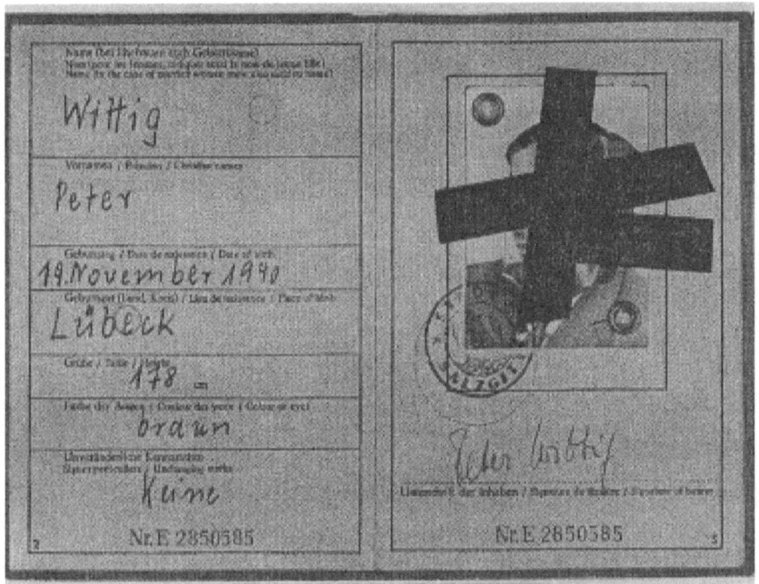

...Fake Passport in the Name of Peter Wittig...

WHEN EAST GERMAN INTELLIGENCE felt an agent's training was complete, the spy was given a fake identity card. I received mine at the beginning of 1969. With the new name, I was also given a new history.

My alias was Peter Wittig. In an emergency, I had to travel as quickly as possible to East Berlin. Peter Wittig was a West German who lived in Salzgitter, East of Lower Saxony, near the GDR border. Like many in his surroundings, he'd worked in a salt mine. He was killed in 1967 in a car accident. His parents were already dead, and he had no brothers or sisters.

Once again, I had to sign a document declaring that I had contact with state authorities in the GDR and had received a West German passport, which was the property of the Ministry of National Defense of the GDR. I was entirely at their mercy by signing this declaration, according to Eberhardt and Heiner.

I committed to memorizing Peter's school and the names of teachers and classmates. I knew which sports club he belonged to and which football team he played for. In retrospect, I'm glad I never had to use this false passport. The photo was of me, but Eberhard had put my data in his messy writing, and my signature was from me.

At signature control, where customs compare the writing of the signature with the data, I would have flunked it.

I knew which sports club he belonged to and which football team he played for. In retrospect, I'm glad I never had to use this false passport. The photo was of me, but Eberhard had put my data in his messy writing, and my signature was from me. At signature control, where customs compare the writing of the signature with the data, I would have flunked it.

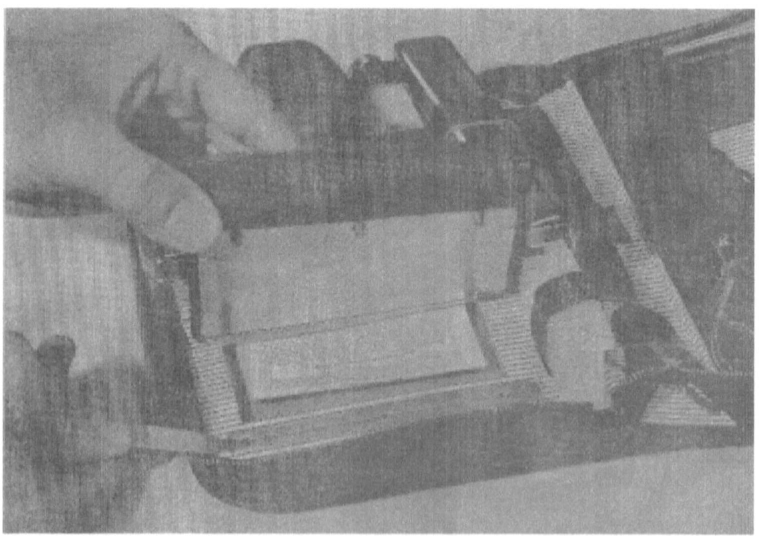

...Above the luxury toilet bag with the hidden spaces...

When I went to Berlin, I kept this passport safe in a travel pouch I'd received from the East Germans. This was intended for overseas travel, but then I used my Dutch passport. During those years, you had to show the card at every border. Still, I didn't need it in the Netherlands because carrying an identity card was optional when one was out.

The fathers were happy with what the East Germans had made available. I'd be even more valuable to them. It also gave them an insight into the progress the East Germans thought I'd made up to that point.

Of course, I admired and photographed the fake passport and travel pouch from every possible angle. Then, I had to show the BVD people how I'd found their hiding place. The travel pouch was in the ideal location.

16. Threatening Letters

It's hard to quit being a spy, not with the BVD and especially not with the East Germans. I handed over to the BVD all kinds of stuff the East Germans had made available to me, but I never got them back to return to the East Germans.

Ebi wanted back the codes, the paper, and the false passport on behalf of the Ministry for State Security. Furthermore, he tried to grill me to discover what I'd told the BVD. Above all, the latter seemed to the BVD not to be such a healthy plan, for that would have meant they knew how they functioned. Apart from that, I would instead not make the mistake of mentioning in East Berlin that Käthe's stepfather had advised me to go to the police in Zeist. Perhaps he would have gotten into trouble because of this.

On a relatively cold day in the spring of 1969, Marga gave birth to our son. Then, she tried harder to coax me to end my espionage activities. The fathers did their best to convince her otherwise, but they didn't have a chance against a determined young mother. She said I was now a father and was responsible for her and our son. She didn't want to risk that her husband would end up in an East German prison cell.

She and my mother were identical; my mother knew I was spying and didn't approve from the outset. Because I suffered from epilepsy, she was always concerned about me. Every wife and mother will understand.

The BVD had told me that they "wouldn't know me" if the East Germans ever arrested me. Then, I'd have to wait until I could return to the Netherlands as part of an exchange of agents, which could take months or even years.

Spies have no protection against being fired, either. It would be stupid for a company to keep an agent sitting in a dark prison on the payroll. In such a case, a spouse would be dependent on social welfare. Social assistance in Holland today only existed in 1968.

When my wife emerged victorious in the debate, the BVD continued to direct me. However, Van der Deugd and Van der Niet always took advantage of an opportunity to tell me how bad they thought it was that I'd ended the collaboration. The BVD said they'd received an insight into the East German Secret Service kitchen through me. On top of everything, they warned me never to go to Eastern Europe. "According to the East Germans, you have just completed your basic training, and you are just beginning to bring them success," said Van der Deugd.

What that meant in real terms could have been more evident to me. Probably the press conferences at NATO and AFCENT and traveling to the maneuvers. "Their investment in you and the material they gave you would be lost," Van der Niet concluded.

The Fathers immediately instructed me to let Ebi know I was quitting my journalistic collaboration. As a reason, I should tell them that my wife had made demands because of the birth of our son. That was the truth.

During Marga's pregnancy, I'd kept both the BVD and the East Germans informed of my intentions. Ebi once told me I should tell Marga nothing about my espionage activities. Still, he probably realized that I didn't follow his order.

I have yet to react to the increasing calls to come to East Berlin. The first letters were friendly but insistent. Mainly, they tried to reclaim the property of the East German State Security Service. After a while came the threatening letters that the BVD had said to expect. They threatened to inform my employer and the Dutch police about my espionage activities for a hostile power. In the Netherlands, this would mean a hefty prison sentence. I read this with a smile because I knew that as long as I didn't set foot in Eastern Europe, the East Germans could do nothing to harm me.

He BVD let the East Germans, especially Ebi and Heiner, sweat over me. They'd undoubtedly lose face among their supervisors because they failed to properly evaluate and supervise a spy.

Below is an excerpt from their last letter:

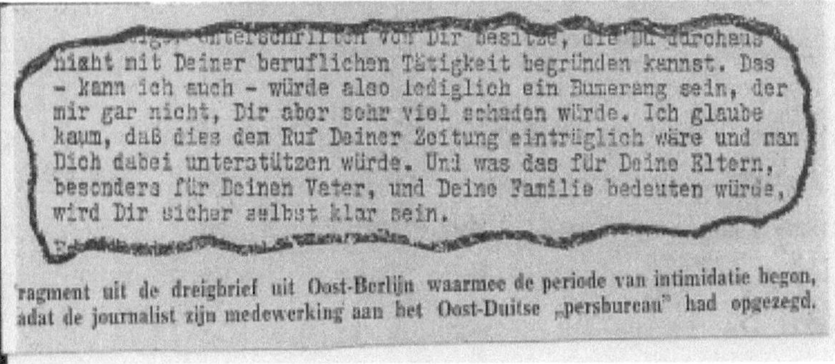

Fragment uit de dreigbrief uit Oost-Berlijn waarmee de periode van intimidatie begon, nadat de journalist zijn medewerking aan het Oost-Duitse „persbureau" had opgezegd.

Translation: *Peter, we have documents confirming that your activities were not aligned with your profession. If we inform your employer and the Dutch police, your attitude might work as a boomerang. I don't think your father will be pleased when that happens.*

At that time, I was still editor of the Nieuwe Zeister Courant. It was taken over by the Utrechts Nieuwsblad, which was part of the Wegener newspaper publishing house. Wegener and the Algemeen Dagblad merged in 2005.

In November 1969, I applied for a job at the Algemeen Dagblad. In my interview with editor-in-chief Huib Appel, I told him that I'd once been a double agent but had ended my involvement with the East Germans due to the birth of our son. That's why I couldn't travel to Eastern Europe for the newspaper. Appel listened without emotion and then said, "Oh, there's not much to be found behind the Iron Curtain, and you're not the first who would be sent to Eastern Europe to write a report." Except for Appel, I'd talked to nobody at the Algemeen Dagblad about this until police reporter René van Eyk interviewed me. (See next chapter.)

The letters continued to arrive from Eberhard, sometimes from Berlin, but mainly from The Hague, where the GDR Embassy was located on Andries Bickerweg.

Fortunately, I no longer lived with my parents because my mother would have been worried by the threats. Marga and I married for over a year and lived on the eleventh floor of a high-rise apartment building in Zeist. When it was foggy, we were literally in the clouds. The building was so high that we could even receive West German television directly. Marga knew that I'd no longer travel to the Eastern Bloc. She trusted everything would be okay and didn't want to discuss it more than necessary.

When Van Eyk's interview with a "real" spy appeared in the Algemeen Dagblad on Saturday, September 26, 1970, the East Germans must have realized that further threats were useless. The BVD used the opportunity to say more than I did. According to the fathers, the interview would end the threatening letters. GDR embassy staff in The Hague read the piece and informed the Ministry of State Security.

Quite a lot has been written about threats from Russia and its allies during the Cold War and about espionage by the GDR and the Soviet Union. However, I was surprised when two months later, at my in-laws' house in Haarlem, I read an article about a Dutch double agent in Panorama who had also been associated with Ebi. The description of the little man matched. The BVD warned me not to say anything to anyone who didn't know of my past espionage activities.

Marga also said the same. She feared that her family would react very emotionally. Her father and mother had died when I started writing this book in 2011. That was notably her request. After she had told her friends about my adventures,

Only in the years after the fall of the Berlin Wall in November 1989 was I allowed to even talk about it among my closest friends. Appel and Van Eyk had passed away before this event. I know nothing about Molzan, but that was his code name. Regardless of my call a few years earlier, he'd never contacted me. I would gladly have reflected on his views of the intelligence service in the GDR in this book.

17. Dutch Daily Interviews a Real Spy

My job at the Algemeen Dagblad was to report on economic and financial matters. I began work on February 1, 1970, and Gerd Selles came three or four months later. René van Eyk was already part of the furniture. Selles also worked in this department. René van Eyk covered police matters. At the start of my first summer at Algemeen Dagblad, Van Eyk trumpeted joyfully that the BVD had offered him five exclusive stories about espionage. This was enough occasion for Selles to boast that he had traveled extensively in Eastern Europe and was familiar with it.

Meanwhile, I tried to determine from the CBS (National Statistics Office) statistical trends in consumer interest in coffee (increasing) and tea (decreasing). I intended to present these trends graphically and ask experts for their opinions. It's nothing spectacular, but I enjoy such challenges as much as a game of chess. Racking my brain sometimes resulted in stories for the paper that were picked up by other news media.

It was in August 1970 that I received the message from my father at the BVD that I was the real spy Van Eyk would have an interview with for his series. The first four articles dealt with various forms of espionage. And now, as a blow to the flare, he got an interview with a real spy. Moreover, he was told he knew that spy.

Van Eyk, already in his fifties, almost danced around the central newsroom, visiting each corner. He proclaimed loudly, "They said I know the person, which means he must work here at the paper because, at the tennis club, we only play older men and women."

Van Eyk was a born journalist, curious about the marrow of his bones. Now, he wanted to find out who his spy was. He put out his antenna in the newsroom and found his man, Gerd Selles, and Selles let him believe. He enjoyed the ruse, and I kept my mouth shut.

On the agreed day, I met one of my fathers at the railway station in The Hague. He took me to a hotel diagonally opposite the Binnenhof (the parliament building in The Hague), where a room had been reserved. I immediately wanted to devour a bowl of biscuits, and a well-filled chocolate box stood on the table, but I had to stop myself for now. I had to wait. First, I got instructions for the conversation and what I could and could not say.

Shortly afterward, Van Eyk, the other father, and a spokesman from the BVD arrived. For a moment, Van Eyk was perplexed and stood with his mouth open at the door. As he was about to speak, he was pushed quickly inside.

Intelligence officers are suspicious; that's part of their job. Eastern bloc spies could have been milling about in the hall.

"You were a spy?" Van Eyk asked incredulously when he saw me.

"You know him?" Van der Niet asked with a smile. Van der Deugd and the other BVD chap laughed when they saw two colleagues facing each other.

"You'd never have guessed," I said to Van Eyk. "Who was your favorite spy?"

Van Eyk asked and mentioned, "Gerd Selles?" Now, I began to laugh as the experienced Van Eyk had gambled on Selles because of his descriptions of the Eastern European trips. "What fun I had when Gerd Selles told us of his Eastern European adventures," I said.

There was a heavy knock on the door, and the BVD people told us to shut up as one of them let the waiter in. "Feel free to order what you want," Van der Deugd said. We didn't need to be told twice since the national treasure guardians were half a mile away. I ordered Hague tea and a plate of miniature pastries. The others ordered beer and something heartier to eat. When the waiter brought everything, a pound of cheese, cut into pieces, was ordered, as Van der Deugd had forgotten to order earlier.

I'd ordered the tea to keep my throat moist while talking, but it was mainly the gentlemen from the BVD who spoke. Of course, Van Eyk also wanted to hear more from me, but he had to form his questions. Then, I was told how to respond. But as soon as I answered in my words, the Fathers took over the answering.

Translation: *"Journalist as a target for spies."*

Van Eyk's full-page article for the Saturday, September 26, 1970, supplement also contained elements not raised during the interview. I asked Van Eyk about it, and he replied, "Peter, the police don't tell you everything;

This interview with my colleague René van Eijk was the final in his series "The Eternal Spy" for the AD daily. The header says: "Journalist as a target for spies."

; even when they ask you to write an article that will help catch criminals, there are always facts they hide in their searches or to take care of; the other side will not hear too much. The Secret Service is worse. Following my instructions, I spoke again with the men from the BVD. I combined the information from both interviews into one article. I had to give this to the BVD to read—one of their conditions for letting me interview a spy. What appears in the papers is a version approved by the BVD."

Van Eyk added that the Fathers justified the censorship by saying that the East Germans should not learn more than they already knew. Corrections by the BVD brought inconsistencies to the article. For example, the journalist came almost too late and, with the help of the police, to the BVD. But thanks to the BVD, no military or other secret has been betrayed to East Germany. From the latter, it was obvious that from the beginning, the BVD had checked documents before I was allowed to take them to East Berlin.

The East Germans at the embassy had no doubt translated the article by Van Eyk on the same weekend, encoded it, and sent it to the Stasi. There were many antenna masts on the roof of the embassy. As a curious journalist, I wondered where all the threatening letters had been sent when I walked past the building. After Van Eyk's interview with the real spy, they must have understood that I was the spy, and the BVD was responsible for its publication in the Algemeen Dagblad.

The day the article was published was my mother's birthday. Just before Marga and I moved to Zeist with our son, my neighbor came running up excitedly, waving a newspaper. "Peter, I think that is you," he shouted. I quickly steered him inside. Of course, I had to deny it. "I could swear that was you. A part of the face is visible. It's about a journalist whose father is also a journalist." The inside of the fake passport showed a picture of my face. BVD had tried to make it unrecognizable. He had been paying attention when we played Yahtzee or Scrabble in the evening. He was genuinely sorry.

In retrospect, Marga and I had to admit he was right because, despite the black bar, enough of my face could be seen for someone to recognize me. If an accountant could recognize me, security people would, too, so my cover could have been better.

It was understandable that my parents returned to the story when we visited my mother on her birthday. My father also discovered differences between the report and the facts as he knew them. My mother was happy that the fuss was now over. And my wife, from the depths of her soul, agreed.

Shortly before, Marga and I met with Van der Niet and Van der Deugd for a farewell dinner. Marga and the men knew each other because, just before our wedding, she was admitted to the hospital for an operation on her appendix. The BVD people visited her and introduced themselves as Peter's friends. Marga was able to get out of bed. They'd taken her to a quiet room, where they told her that I had a side job as a BVD double agent and, therefore, had to travel to East Berlin now and again. Of course, they told her that there was little or no risk to her future husband because the great BVD supervised him. Marga was surprised and annoyed that I hadn't told her anything.

At dinner, I could tell them when Van Eyk's article would be published. They told me what they'd done with the article, but I knew that already from Van Eyk. It was only later that I saw how much they had changed things. The men warned us that we should contact them directly.

Suppose we heard anything from Berlin or the Embassy in The Hague. That did not happen.

18. My Name Appears in Stasi Files

In an emotional address on TV and radio in October 1990, then-Chancellor Helmut Kohl announced the official union of East and West Germany and the related conditions. Meanwhile, the wages in East Germany would remain low. Still, West Germans would pay a "solidarity supplement" tax to reconstruct the eastern part of the new Federal Republic. The extra tax revenue was urgently needed.

According to world trade statistics, in the 1980s, the GDR reached seventeenth place among the industrialized nations, but this seemed a bitter disappointment. Under Honecker's rule, half of the national revenue went to the army and the occupying Russian forces, financing the enormous apparatus of the State Security Service and political propaganda.

After I had related my experiences to my acquaintances, the question of whether my name was somewhere in the Stasi archives began to gnaw at me. For inquiries about the Stasi, an investigator with a large team headed by a Federal Commissioner was appointed. The archive contains millions of names. Everything was filed about all known GDR citizens, from their marital status to health records, family relationships, hobbies, interests, and even their knowledge of domestic and foreign affairs.

The GDR crawled with Stasi informers, so family allegiances were always casual. No one said anything that could be used against them, sometimes not even within the family. This was thanks to Erich and Margot Honecker, who, in many issues, was the "evil genius" behind her husband.

This was especially true of security. Schools, factories, and institutions were swarming with informers.

Furthermore, in the West, everyone had to offer something in exchange for information. They had their people in almost all State institutions at national and municipal levels and large companies such as chemical producers. Espionage was not limited to political and military affairs; industrial processes and their secrets were also of interest to spies.

The number of spies in other countries was relatively limited. Still, the East Germans also sniffed around in communist "brother" countries. Germans, particularly those in the former GDR, increasingly requested information about their names and those of their family, colleagues, sports friends, and girlfriends or boyfriends.

I would instead not jump the queue, so it was only in May 1996 that I wrote a letter requesting information about my name and anything related. In addition, I asked if they could provide me with information about a man known to me as Eberhard Molzan. I'd have loved to have had a coffee or beer with him and reflected on our experiences between 1967 and 1970.

All the Federal Commissioner could find was a card with my name on it. It was in the Stasi archive of the military, foreign Secret Service, and the HVA (Foreign Administration). In the last months of 1989, the HVA had thoroughly destroyed its archive shortly after the Wall's fall. Additional information was probably gathered by the East German Ministry for Disarmament and Defense in the summer of 1990 before the official union of the two countries in October.

The Federal Commissioner wrote me a letter confirming my name was found in the Stasi archives. He points out that immediately after the Berlin Wall fell, the East German Ministry of State Security decided the espionage department should dissolve itself and burn all documents. That was, in particular, to protect the tens of thousands of informants in West Germany. He had not found any facts about an HVA spy named Eberhard Molzan.

Epilogue

My name in the Stasi archives was the extra proof that I had been a Western informant (contact person) for the Reconnaissance Administration (HVA), the foreign intelligence department of the Ministry for State Security (MfS, or Stasi). The HVA staff, whom I knew as Eberhard and Heiner, had the rank of officer in the People's Army (the military) of the GDR. After the Israeli Mossad, they considered themselves the best intelligence service in the world.

They were required to show higher deployment, flexibility, and commitment than other employees of the Stasi and, of course, unconditional loyalty and dedication to the Marxist-Leninist doctrine and the party policies of the Socialist Unity Party of Germany (SED).

On the one hand, the HVA selected, examined, and accompanied HVA foreigners who worked as spies or informants in their country. Usually, these people were called "contacts." In a particular category are today's lover boys, called Romeo agents in the 1960s, whose task it was to seduce the secretaries of highly regarded West German politicians. The Stasi called them "intimate companions."

The selected secretaries were not married. If necessary, the Stasi agent had to enter into a marriage of convenience with her. Getting information justified the means.

The training of both groups usually took years. East Germans were selected to spy abroad due to their education (high school or technical college) and were given intensive training. This could be about a field of study but also about flawlessly learning a language and accent, the culture, and the history of the area where they went. Learning about several pseudonyms and their associated history and education was always challenging. They had to read regional newspapers and belong to a club to be assimilated into their new environment, making it easier for them to gather information.

HVA's espionage was directed primarily at West Germany and neutral European countries such as Switzerland, Austria, and Sweden. De Britse's intelligence leaked like a sieve, and many Britons wanted to earn something extra. This made it easy for the HVA to contact many Britons for information on the defense of their country. In other European countries, there was more interest in information about NATO. In all Western European countries, the HVA supported peace movements. The IKV (Inner Church Peace Association) was indirectly supported and infiltrated in the Netherlands to instigate actions, demonstrations, and anti-NATO material for the rest of the world.

The Russian KGB did not allow the East Germans to spy in America. They wanted to collect intelligence and feared that the CIA would easily expose HVA contacts. They feared that Russian interests could be damaged.

The HVA supplied most of the countries in Eastern Europe (excluding Russia) with intelligence acquired through espionage, both military and political. Information from industrial espionage obtained by the HVA was primarily used in the East German factories and technological and industrial research institutes.

It was good for my health that during the Cold War, I never visited Eastern Europe after terminating my relationship with the HVA and

BVD. An arrest warrant with a photo was issued throughout Eastern Europe for everyone who stopped cooperating with Eastern European security services. As I had given their possessions to counterintelligence (in my case, the BVD), I'd have been at the mercy of East Germany.

Western spy hunters knew the consequences of their lack of proper controls. West Germany was open to everyone from East Germany, so the borders needed to be checked. Spies could effortlessly be dropped, but traveling from West to East took much work.

The Stasi did not allow any Westerners in Berlin. One could only get a day pass to visit East Berlin. For every other visit, a visa was needed. The West German immigration policy for immigrants from "oppressed Eastern States" was very lenient. On no occasion did anyone in West Berlin stop me, let alone question me. My passport was examined once.

On the other hand, it was extremely difficult for Western intelligence agencies, especially after the construction of the Wall in 1961, to spy on the East. With a day's pass, you can stay in Berlin for almost one day. If you wanted to stay longer in the GDR, you required a visa.

The HVA's end arrived shortly after the fall of the Wall in November 1989, with the nationwide storming of local offices. Then, it took almost eleven months before the Federal Republic could take the GDR under its wing. By the end of November 1989, the leadership of the HVA, the Stasi, and the Central Committee of the Communist Party decided that the HVA had to dissolve itself.

At the end of February 1990, thousands of enraged East Germans stormed the Ministry. Still, they left the offices of the HVA located there untouched. They believe no systematic interference in their privacy had been spied out or betrayed. East Germans knew that the Espionage Service had no eye on them; they were after the archives to find out which of their family, friends, and colleagues had spied on them for the Stasi. At the end of June 1990, almost all personal documents were destroyed in the vast HVA archive. Therefore, the number of employees in the last six months has increased by four hundred.

In Closing

I wish to express my thanks to the following people who helped me write this book:

My *wife Marga* (deceased) and friend Käthe

My *father and mother* (deceased)

The stepfather and mother of Käthe (deceased) and her sister Angela

My *"father's" at the BVD* (probably deceased).

Gudrun and her husband in Berlin

The East German agent supervisors, *Eberhard Molzan and Heiner,* did not react to the appeal published on Neues Deutschland's front page and did not contact me.

Herman Broekhuizen and Gerrit den Braber (AVRO, both deceased)

Algemeen Dagblad Crime editor *René van Eyk* (deceased)

Margot Honecker (deceased)

All others who played a small or significant role in this book.

Käthe married two years after I did. Like us, she has two children, a boy and a girl. And just like us, they have moved due to her husband's work.

Margot Honecker lived in political asylum in Chile until she died in May 2016, broke. Nazis fled there and to other South American countries after the Second World War. She has not returned to

Germany for fear of being arrested and having to answer for her actions. She believed until her death that they had the best intentions for the GDR and that Marxist-Leninism would finally prevail in a perfect world. Before she and her husband left Germany in 1989–1990, they took refuge in the church, which they had persecuted when they were in power. Erich returned to Germany at some point, was arrested, and went to jail. After it became apparent that he was seriously ill, he was, for humanitarian reasons, allowed to return to Margot.

During our second encounter, Gudrun had written down my address in Zeist. Still, I am waiting to hear from her or Hermann again.

Writing this book has been like sitting on an egg for years before it hatched. The parts about the East German orders, when they wanted to ensure my safety, to get in somewhere, or to take pictures, have generated much merriment at gatherings and festivities. I've had such fun writing this book.

I have a property, probably early recognized by the BVD, that my subconscious, in critical moments, sets off my emotions. That might have been the case with near accidents in cars and planes that I have experienced. To date, I have acted the right way.

Hopefully, you found the reading interesting. Of course, you can learn a lot from it, such as how to trust your advisors and, not least, your logic. You must stay calm, let others talk, and shut your mouth.

I've changed the names of everyone still alive or if I don't know if they're dead or alive. Even the gentlemen from the BVD introduced themselves with names different from those I used in the book.

I also hope you share my opinion that I cared much more about my father, Käthe's stepfather, and my BVD fathers than the Stasi guys. I was not the only Dutchman who could fool them with the help of the BVD. We Dutch might not be as crazy as Double Dutch suggests.

THANK YOU FOR READING this book. I hope you now have a more profound understanding of the communists' aggressive thinking and how stupid they might be. I also hope you smile about it.

The final article on 9-26-1970 in the series "The Eternal Spy" related to me. The header says: "Journalist as a target for spies."

Peter

The Author, Peter van Wermeskerken

P eter was born on December 31, 1939, at 7.30 a.m. Two hours later, he came unexpectedly to his brother. At the end of World War II, he was diagnosed with epilepsy. This had a significant negative impact on his education. Yet, he was the best at writing essays at school. As a 14-year-old, Peter wrote his first reports for his father's local newspaper. It didn't take long before he also started journalism. Through several newspapers, he eventually came to AD in Rotterdam, the second-largest national daily in Holland. After coming here, he specialized in energy and macroeconomics. Later, he became chief of the economics desk. After retirement, he volunteered as a legal advisor and municipal councilor with the Refugee Aid. He was a youth coach at his chess club. Peter married in 1968 and had two children with his wife. She died in 2014. Four years later, he remarried a woman from Vietnam. They live in The Hague, Holland. His first wife set him up in 2011 to write about his years as a double agent.

That triggered me to write more, particularly fiction in very different genres.

More from this Publisher

Reed Sailing, an erotic novel e-book, US$6.99

This is an erotic novel, partly based on the author's own experiences. During a test for treatment for his epilepsy, he meets a girl. It's love at first sight. Their first months are pretty turbulent. A week of sailing makes them calmer; they learn to work together, both with sailing and caring for each other. She is going to help him prepare for an exam. When his former boss, Jan, becomes ill, they temporarily run the farm for him. In this way, they work towards a wedding in a few years. But it would never come to that.

Mike & Alex, the Defenders of the Animal Forest (smashwords.com) US$ 2.99

As you thought already, this is a children's book. It's about successful actions by animals against nasty people. It's educational about the behavior and way many animals, both from the farm and the forest, live. The author is working on follow-ups.

A Kid During WWII Wartime (From Sabotage to Survival to Liberation) (smashwords.com) US$ 1.99

These are four short stories from my early childhood. The Germans imprisoned my father. Therefore, I sabotaged five army cars. We ate potato peel soup with sand and five army cars. We ate potato peel soup with sand (that rubs the stomach)—two more stories.

Reviews of the original book

Thank you for sharing such a detailed and fascinating part of your life. I read the material immediately, and I was hooked on your adventure. I love the book. And I enjoyed your honest and riveting story. For me, it was very educational. Many of the stories you described were like reading the best espionage thriller. Well done

Joanna M. Valius, Literary Agent, York, UK

"Peter is a wonderful writer and great to work with!" Ellen Green, AEG Publishing, Houston, Texas press manager.

Double Agent is more than just the story of a young Dutch journalist recruited by East German agents to smuggle information to them during the height of the Cold War and then being recruited to filter that information through the Dutch Secret Service. The story reveals the depth of control a totalitarian state like the GDR had over its citizens. Double Spy also clearly illustrated the price the GDR paid to maintain its depth of control.

Peter takes the East Germans on a merry ride through NATO and the West, telling and showing them exactly what they want to hear and see. Peter stops the East German handlers' repetition of their instructions to him and corrects them. He tells them all he has to do is act naturally, but only then does Peter and the reader realize that the spy handlers don't know what acting naturally means. Peter even defied instructions that clearly showed the handlers had no idea of life in the West beyond what their government told them. Double Agent is more than just a story of Cold War espionage and counter-espionage; Double Spy illustrates how oppressed the oppressors must be to maintain their hold over their people.

Don C. Ciers US Army (Retired)

Author of The Enlightenment Protocols

www.ingramcontent.com/pod-product-compliance
Lightning Source LLC
Chambersburg PA
CBHW021447150726
47989CB00001B/429